Very early in the war the German army high command realised that the 8.8cm gun, initially designed as an anti-aircraft weapon, was capable of effectively neutralising any of the current generation of enemy tanks and very probably the next. Searching for a suitable platform for the gun, the German army's ordnance department, or Heereswaffenamt, in early August 1942, requested that the firm of Friedrich Krupp AG submit designs for a new Jagdpanzer, or tank destroyer, and stipulated that the vehicle was to be armed with the 8.8cm gun and based on the chassis of the Panther, which was at that time under development but had not gone into production (1). In 1939 Krupp had been asked to design a fully-tracked assault gun mounting the 8.8cm Flak L/56, which the designers had proposed to mount on the chassis of a Pzkw IV (2).

Quite probably reluctant to drop work on their heavy Sturmgeschütz, the Krupp designers claimed that they could not complete the construction drawings for the new Jagdpanzer before January 1943. As the Heereswaffenamt specification called for the first vehicle was to be ready by June 1943, with full-scale production beginning in the next month, it was decided that Daimler-Benz would take over the design development as production was, in any case, to be undertaken at that company's Berlin-Marienfelde plant (3). The basic shape of the new vehicle was the same as the Panther II tank, which was also under development at the time. The initial designation was 8.8cm Panzerjäger 43/3 (L/71) auf Panther Fahrgestell and the Heereswaffenamt requested that the first hulls be ready by mid-1943 (4).

However, after a considerable amount of work had been completed on the Jagdpanzer project, it was decided in May 1943 to suspend development of the Panther II and Daimler-Benz was ordered

to redesign their prototype arou components of the Panther I, wh that time was just going into servic was a significant change and mear among other things, a new susp had to be incorporated into the desi_.. ___ that the armour was reduced all round with the front plate now of 80mm thickness while the hull sides, hull rear plate and the superstructure rear were decreased to 40mm. At the same time it was decided that the firm of Mülhenbau und Industrie AG (MIAG) would take over the detailed design as Daimler-Benz was experiencing its own production problems. The agreement that MIAG would produce the finished design had in fact been reached in the previous December. The new design team made further reductions in the armour thickness in an effort to reduce weight and a Heereswaffenamt amendment of 9 June 1943, increased the crew to six with the introduction of a radio operator (5).

A full-scale wooden model that Daimler-Benz had completed was handed over to MIAG and used as a guide for the assembly drawings (6). On 23 October 1943 the model was shown to Hitler together with wooden versions of what would become the Tiger II and Jagdtiger. After approval of the design, the first trial production vehicle was completed at MIAG within weeks. The first vehicles of the production series left the assembly plant in January 1944, just two months behind schedule, with a further seven completed in the following month. The first vehicles were delivered to combat units in April 1944 and by the end of the war almost 420 Jagdpanthers had been assembled.

In early June 1944 the most powerful tank destroyer produced during the Second World War was waiting at the training grounds of Mailly-le-Camp in France to make its combat debut.

_...._ .u...... .. .._ book in this series *Panther Tanks. Germany Army and Waffen SS, Normandy Campaign 1944.*

2. At that time the heaviest German tank available.

3. Krupp would, however, continue work on the gun and gun mounts.

4. This was in fact the title mentioned in a Waffenamt document dated 1 May 1943. By February 1945 the vehicle had been referred to by at least eighteen different names with Jagdpanther G1 being the last.

5. This number was reduced to five on the production vehicle.

6. The project was by now designated mittlere Panzerjäger mit 8.8cm L/71 auf Panther.

Photographed in one of the MNH assembly halls at Hannover in May 1945, these Jagdpanthers and a single Panther sit next to a row of Maybach HL230 P30 engines. The armoured hulls, or Panzerwanne, were all welded together by the Brandenburger Eisenwerke and sent to either MIAG in Braunschweig, MNH at Hannover or MBA near Berlin for final assembly.

Hamburg

Emden

Bremen

Berlin

Hannover

Brunswick

Amsterdam

HOLLAND

Magdeburg

Rotterdam

Arnhem

Kassel

Leipzig

London

Nijmegen

Erfurt

Dover

Ostend

Antwerp

Dusseldorf

Portsmouth

Dunkirk

Ghent

Maastricht

Cologne

GERMANY

Calais

Brussels

Duren

Lille

BELGIUM

Spa

Bonn

Abbeville

Malmedy

Coblenz

Cherbourg

Dieppe

St. Quentin

Bastogne

St. Vith

Frankfurt

Schweinfurt

Le Havre

Amiens

Sedan

Trier

Mainz

Carentan

Rouen

Compiegne

Luxembourg

Fürth

St. Lô

Caen

Vernon

Reims

Verdun

Thionville

Saarbrücken

Regensburg

Avranches

Dreux

Paris

Chalons

Commercy

Metz

Argentan

Remilly

Nancy

Strasbourg

Ulm

Munich

Chartres

St. Dizier

Epinal

Augsburg

Le Mans

Chateaudun

Troyes

Chaumont

Colmar

Orleans

Chatillon

Belfort

Basel

AUSTRIA

Dijon

Nantes

Tours

Sombernon

Besancon

SWITZERLAND

Nevers

Autun

Berne

ITALY

FRANCE

Cluny

Vichy

Lyon

Vienne

Etienne

Grenoble

Turin

Valence

Biancon

Bologna

Bordeaux

Livron

Genoa

Montelimar

Avignon

Florence

Nice

Pisa

Toulouse

Cannes

Sete

Marseilles

Toulon

With the Allied breakout from Normandy in July and August 1944 the front moved rapidly eastwards and by mid-September ran from just north of Ostend along the Dutch-Belgian border to Maastricht, then south to the outskirts of Aachen. From there the line ran south through Luxembourg, following the Moselle through Thionville, then continuing south to the east of Epinal and Belfort before turning sharply towards the Swiss frontier. By 16 December 1944, and the commencement of Wacht am Rhein, the Americans had overrun most of Alsace and Lorraine and the British and Canadians had advanced as far as Nijmegen in the north. The latter was, however, the ground gained during Operation Market Garden in late September and the centre of the front remained basically unchanged. The national borders depicted here are those of 1945 and although I have endeavoured to use the correct contemporary place names throughout the text, anglicised versions are shown here. The timeline below illustrates the most significant events of the campaign from the invasion until the German surrender.

6 June 1944. Allied troops land on the Normandy beaches as part of Operation Overlord. Although the landings are largely successful, a number of important first-day objectives, including the town of Caen, remain in German hands.

7 June 1944. The British resume their efforts to capture Caen but are unsuccessful. German counterattacks are stopped by naval gunfire less than 5 kilometres from the invasion beaches. Elsewhere, the Germans are able to deny Carpiquet airfield, to the west of Caen, to the Canadians.

8 June 1944. British and American units link up north of Bayeux.

9 June 1944. The Luftwaffe attacks British positions at Lion-sur-Mer and also attempts to destroy the Orne bridges. As night falls, the tanks of Panzer-Lehr-Division reach the front north-west of Caen.

10 June 1944. German units abandon the town of Tilly-sur-Seulles although it is recaptured the next day.

12 June 1944. Despite local German successes, British and US Army units are able to link up near Carentan creating a continuous front.

13 June 1944. Elements of British 7th Armoured Division are severely mauled at Villers-Bocage by a platoon of Tiger I tanks from schwere SS-Panzer-Abteilung 101.

14 June 1944. US troops complete the capture of Carentan.

15 June 1944. The fighting for Tilly-sur-Seulles continues with the tanks of Panzer-Regiment 6 added to the defence.

18 June 1944. Over the next two days, Panzer-Regiment 3 and Panzer Regiment 6 are involved in heavy fighting around Tilly-sur-Seulles.

20 June 1944. The first Jagdpanthers of 1.Kompanie, schwere Panzerjäger-Abteilung 654 arrive at the front.

25 June 1944. The British commence Operation Epsom, an attempt to outflank the German defenders of Caen and secure the city. After two days of costly fighting Caen remains in German hands.

27 June 1944. One company of schwere Panzerjäger-Abteilung 654 with eight operational vehicles, is attached to Panzer-Lehr-Division. On the same day, tanks of the British 11th Armoured Division overrun much of Hill 112, the highest point on the Normandy battlefield, south-west of Caen. Later that day a determined counterattack is made and the summit is occupied by the Germans as night falls.

29 June 1944. Suspecting that a strong counterattack is imminent, all British armoured units around Hill 112 withdraw, allowing the Germans to occupy the area without loss.

1 July 1944. Oberbefehlshaber West orders that the Panzer units around Caen be gradually transferred to the west to meet the expected American offensive. To the British and Canadians, however, Caen remains the focus of attention.

2 July 1944. The Panzer-Lehr-Division is withdrawn from the front line and moved towards the south-east in anticipation of a major American attack. The Jagdpanthers remain in the area around Caen.

9 July 1944. British and Canadian units fight their way into Caen and manage to secure the northern suburbs although the Germans stubbornly cling to the southern half.

10 July 1944. A major British offensive captures Hill 112 after heavy fighting.

11 July 1944. The Jagdpanthers of schwere Panzerjäger-Abteilung 654 go into action for the first time. One vehicle is disabled by friendly fire and later recovered. A German counterattack drives the British from the summit of Hill 112. On the same day US troops enter St. Lô.

16 July 1944. A Kampfgruppe under Oberst Traugott Köhn, the commander of Panzer-Regiment 130, launchs a counterattack to the west of Villers-Bocage. The Germans are beaten back with heavy loss, including Oberst Köhn who is killed.

18 July 1944. In a single day of fighting around Bouguébus the British and Canadians lose 100 tanks.

19 July 1944. Canadian units clear the southern suburbs of Caen. British tanks enter Bras and Hubert-Folie on the outskirts of the town.

20 July 1944. At Rastenburg in East Prussia, an attempt is made on Hitler's life.

25 July 1944. The US Army's Operation Cobra begins. The Americans advance rapidly towards their objectives.

28 July 1944. American units capture Coutances, about 40 kilometres west of St.-Lô, but are held up outside the town by a Kampfgruppe made up from 2.SS-Panzer-Division and 17.SS-Panzergrenadier-Division.

A Jagdpanther of schwere Panzerjäger-Abteilung 559 photographed while the battalion was in training. This vehicle has the two-piece gun barrel introduced into production in May 1944 and the single driver's periscope on the glacis

Photographed in Elbeuf on 28 August 1944 this Jagdpanther of 1.Kompanie, schwere Panzerjäger-Abteilung 654, commanded by Feldwebel Siebels, was destroyed by its crew after they failed to access a crossing of the River Oissel.

30 July 1944. *Three Jagdpanthers of schwere Panzerjäger-Abteilung 654 destroy almost a full company of British Churchill tanks in a brief action near Bois du Homme.*

31 July 1944. *The first total loss of a Jagdpanther on the Normandy front is reported.*

4 August 1944. *Hill 112 is occupied by British units after the German defenders abandon their positions. With the evacuation of Caen the hill no longer has any strategic significance.*

6 August 1944. *Just before midnight, the Germans launch Operation Lüttich, an ambitious attack intended to blunt the US Army's Cobra offensive and retake Avranches. Aided by the weather, the Panzers make some early tactical gains, including the capture of Mortain. However, they are met by scores of Allied fighter-bombers by mid-morning.*

8 August 1944. *The battlegroups which had advanced past Mortain towards Saint-Hilaire-du-Harcouët, find themselves in danger of encirclement. On the same day the British launch Operation Totalise with fresh Canadian and Polish units which attack towards Falaise. That afternoon, the Americans occupy Le Mans, the headquarters of SS-Oberstgruppenführer Paul Hausser's 7.Armee.*

9 August 1944. *Supported by the last Tigers of schwere SS-Panzer-Abteilung 101, the tanks of SS-Panzer-Regiment 12 begin an assault north-east of Falaise. The Germans claim the destruction of twenty-eight Canadian tanks without loss.*

11 August 1944. *In an attempt to cut off the German units withdrawing after Operation Lüttich, the British mount an attack towards Moncy on the Vire to Saint-Germain-du-Crioult road. Meeting fierce resistance, the attack bogs down after advancing just 800 metres.*

13 August 1944. *The last German units withdraw from Mortain.*

14 August 1944. *Tanks of SS-Panzer-Regiment 12 halt an Allied advance just north of Falaise but are forced from their positions as darkness falls on the following day.*

17 August 1944. *Canadian troops enter Falaise threatening the German army in Normandy with encirclement.*

19 August 1944. *Polish armoured units link up with US troops at Chambois just south of Mont Ormel as evening approaches.*

20 August 1944. *During the early morning, the remaining tanks of SS-Panzer-Regiment 2 and SS-Panzer-Regiment 9 mount an attack towards the Polish positions on Mont Ormel. By noon another Kampfgruppe manages to break through the Polish front as Canadian reinforcements are prevented from reaching the battle. Within a few hours approximately 10,000 Germans are able to escape from the Falaise Pocket.*

21 August 1944. *During the early evening Polish and Canadian troops meet at Coudehard, north-east of Trun, closing the German escape route for the last time.*

25 August 1944. *Allied units enter Paris, the final objective of Operation Overlord.*

30 August 1944. *The last German troops cross the Seine leaving much of their heavy equipment behind. The battle for Normandy is over.*

6 September 1944. *The first Jagdpanthers of schwere Panzerjäger-Abteilung 559 arrive at Utrecht in Holland and are immediately directed towards the front.*

8 September 1944. *Elements of schwere Panzerjäger-Abteilung 559 support two battalions of Fallschirmjäger defending Wijchmal, east of Geel, in Belgium.*

11 September 1944. *Due to production delays, Hitler orders that heavy Panzerjäger battalions will henceforth be made up of one company of Jagdpanthers and two companies of Sturmgeschütz III assault guns and later Jagdpanzer IV tank destroyers.*

29 September 1944. *The commander of schwere Panzerjäger-Abteilung 559 reports that just three operational Jagdpanthers are available for deployment.*

30 September 1944. *Hauptmann Friedrich Lüders, a company commander of schwere Panzerjäger-Abteilung 654, is awarded the Ritterkreuz.*

1 October 1944. *The last vehicles of schwere Panzerjäger-Abteilung 519 are unloaded at the front.*

6 October 1944. *Oberfeldwebel August Kaminski, a platoon commander of schwere Panzerjäger-Abteilung 655, is awarded the Ritterkreuz.*

8 October 1944. *The crews of schwere Panzerjäger-Abteilung 560, which had been training at Mielau since April, receive their first four Jagdpanthers.*

21 October 1944. *Aachen is captured, earning the distinction of being the first German city to fall to the Western Allies.*

28 October 1944. *All eligible Germans are ordered to enrol in the Volkssturm or face court-martial.*

31 October 1944. *British units reach the river Maas, south of Rotterdam, and establish a bridgehead.*

1 November 1944. *British units land on Walcheren in the Scheldt Estuary.*

2 November 1944. *US Army units move to attack the Roer Dams along the German-Belgian frontier, opposed by remnants of a single German infantry division.*

4 November 1944. *Elements of 116.Panzer-Division begin a series of counterattacks against US units in the Roer dam region. Within 48 hours a surprise assault breaks the US defences at Vossenack.*

7 November 1944. *Schwere Panzerjäger-Abteilung 519 is attached to 116.Panzer-Division as part of Kamfgruppe Bayer. On the same day the battle group recaptures Kommerscheidt.*

9 November 1944. *The last German units on Walcheren surrender. The Moerdijk bridgehead across the Meuse river is evacuated.*

10 November 1944. *The first Volkssturm unit goes into action in the west.*

11 November 1944. *The Jagdpanthers of schwere Panzerjäger-Abteilung 559 are attached to Panzer-Lehr-Division, replacing I.Abteilung, Panzer-Regiment 130 in preparation for the upcoming Ardennes offensive. On the same day, German 1.Armee headquarters leaves Metz as US units capture three bridgeheads over the Moselle.*

16 November 1944. *US Army units launch an attack to the east of Aachen.*

17 November 1944. *German units counterattack towards Puffendorf south-east of Geilenkircken. On the following day, units of the US 3rd Army cross the German frontier. Metz is now cut off.*

19 November 1944. *US units fight their way into the suburbs of Metz. The French 1st Armoured Division reaches the Rhine. German units counterattack near Merzenhausen and around Tripsrath north of Geilenkircken.*

23 November 1944. *Elements of 12.Volksgrenadier-Division attempt to retake Pützlohn supported by the Tigers of Panzer-Abteilung (Funklenk) 301 using remotely-controlled demolition carriers.*

24 November 1944. *The Allies cross the River Saar near the German border.*

28 November 1944. *The US 9th Army reaches the Roer.*

30 November 1944. *Schwere Panzerjäger-Abteilung 653 claims to have destroyed fifty-two enemy tanks and damaged another nine in the last ten days of fighting.*

3 December 1944. *The first Jagdpanthers of schwere Panzerjäger-Abteilung 560 leave the training grounds at Mielau for the front.*

8 December 1944. *The last elements of schwere Panzerjäger-Abteilung 560 are unloaded at Niederhausen and prepare to move to the front. German troops evacuate Jülich on the Roer river.*

This Panzerbefehlswagen Jagdpanther of Stab, schwere Panzerjäger-Abteilung 559 was photographed near Geel, east of Antwerp, after the fighting for the Albert Canal in September 1944. Note the armoured cover for the Sternantenna insulator on the superstructure rear on the left-hand side. Another command vehicle of this battalion is shown in the photographs on page 13 and in the illustration section on page 19.

This Jagdpanther, built by MNH in December 1944, was captured by the US Army during the Ardennes Offensive. In 1946 it was sent to the Army Ordnance Museum in Aberdeen, Maryland where it remains to this day, although its original camouflage scheme has unfortunately been worn and covered with successive coats of grey paint.

9 December 1944. Hauptmann Erwin Kressmann, the commander of 1.Kompanie schwere Panzerjäger-Abteilung 519, is awarded the Ritterkreuz for his actions during the fighting in the Hürtgenwald in November. On the same day, thirty-one Panzer IV 70(V) tank destroyers of schwere Panzerjäger-Abteilung 655 arrive at the front, having left the Jagdpanther company at Mielau.

13 December 1944. German 7.Armee withdraws into the fortified positions of the Westwall.

15 December 1944. The commander of schwere Panzerjäger-Abteilung 519 reports that just five serviceable Jagdpanthers are available for the offensive which is due to begin within hours.

16 December 1944. The German Army launches Wacht am Rhein, the last major operation in the west. Achieving complete surprise, the German offensive manages to break through the American lines on a 70-mile front. However, difficult terrain and poor weather hamper the German units and ominously none reach their assigned first-day objectives.

17 December 1944. In the early morning the Germans reach Schönberg, 10 kilometres from St Vith. An armoured Kampfgruppe under SS-Obersturmbannführer Joachim Peiper thrusts past Buchholz while 12.Volksgrenadier-Division takes Losheimergraben.

18 December 1944. Kampfgruppe Peiper reaches La Gleize and brings Chauveheid under attack. After several attempts to capture Krinkett, the Germans bypass the town. After less than 48 hours the headquarters of both 6.Armee and 5.Armee report shortages of fuel.

19 December 1944. US units come under attack at Dom Bütgenbach, less than 10 kilometres east of Malmedy. On the following morning units of 6.Armee capture Stavelot.

21 December 1944. Although US Army units retake Stavelot, Bastogne is besieged and 5.Armee captures St. Vith while the attacks on Dom Bütgenbach continue.

22 December 1944. Kampfgruppe von Böhm, formed around the reconnaissance battalion of 2.Panzer-Division, breaches the American line and advances towards Buissonville and Achene.

24 December 1944. Troops of Kampfgruppe Poschinger, made up of units from Panzer-Lehr-Division, enter Rochefort by stealth and after heavy fighting take the town. Buissonville is retaken by the Americans.

25 December 1944. The tanks of 2.Panzer-Division are halted just four miles from the river Meuse. Kampfgruppe von Böhm is surrounded and destroyed despite a relief effort carried out by units of 9.Panzer-Division. On the following day Bastogne is relieved.

30 December 1944. German units launch a heavy attack on the Bastogne corridor. The British attack on Houffalize, north-east of Bastogne, is halted by determined German resistance.

31 December 1944. Heeresgruppe G and Oberkommando Oberrhein launch Operation Nordwind, an attack towards Strasbourg in the Saar valley. The main assault is led by 17.SS-Panzergrenadier-Division and 36.Volksgrenadier-Division with schwere Panzerjäger-Abteilung 654.

3 January 1945. Allied counterattacks begin on the northern side of the Ardennes salient.

5 January 1945. With Operation Nordwind bogged down, a supplementary operation codenamed Sonnenwende begins and units of Oberkommando Oberrhein manage to create a bridgehead on the Rhine between Strasbourg and Hagenau.

6 January 1945. Major Karl-Heinz Noak, the commander of schwere Panzerjäger-Abteilung 654, is awarded the German Cross in Gold.

9 January 1945. Kampfgruppe Feuchtinger launches an attack against Hatten, south of Oldenburg. This action is virtually the last gasp of Operation Nordwind.

12 January 1945. Operation Nordwind is halted 13 miles from Strasbourg. British and US Army forces link up near La-Roche-en-Ardenne, north-west of Houffalize.

13 January 1945. *Leutnant Günther Heyn, as acting commander of 2.Kompanie, schwere Panzerjäger-Abteilung 654, is awarded the German Cross in Gold*

16 January 1945. *10.SS-Panzer-Division spearheads the drive south from Lauterbourg through Seltz, 2 miles west of the Rhine River, in an attempt to seize the Gambsheim bridgehead.*

22 January 1945. *Units of Heeresgruppe G and Oberkommando Öberrhein link up but are unable to force a crossing of the Moder River.*

25 January 1945. *Jagdpanthers of schwere Panzerjäger-Abteilung 654 take part in the defence of Jebsheim in the Colmar Pocket.*

28 January 1945. *The Germans withdraw from the Ardennes salient.*

4 February 1945. *The last German troops leave Belgium.*

5 February 1945. *After fighting in the Rhine-Brückenkopf area, schwere Panzerjäger-Abteilung 560 prepares to leave for the Eastern Front.*

7 February 1945. *The Germans destroy the floodgates in the Ruhr valley in the area west of Cologne, preventing the use of assault bridges.*

8 February 1945. *British and Canadian troops launch an offensive into the Reichswald.*

9 February 1945. *The last Rhine bridge is destroyed in the Colmar Pocket after much of 19.Armee has been evacuated.*

10 February 1945. *US units capture the last of the Ruhr dams.*

12 February 1945. *British and Canadian troops capture Cleve.*

17 February 1945. *US 3rd Army breaks through the Siegfried Line and advances into Germany.*

23 February 1945. *US 9th Army attacks from the Roer bridgehead towards the Hürtgen Forest but is bogged down in savage fighting.*

24 February 1945. *A total of six Jagdpanthers are sent to schwere Panzerjäger-Abteilung 654, although there is no confirmation of their arrival. These were the last vehicles allocated to the battalion before the end of the war.*

28 February 1945. *US units in the Hürtgen Forest break through near Erkelenz, west of Cologne, at great cost.*

2 March 1945. *Schwere Panzerjäger-Abteilung 655 is attached to Division Bayerlein, under 15.Armee.*

6 March 1945. *Cologne surrenders.*

7 March 1945. *The Rhine bridge at Remagen is captured intact.*

10 March 1945. *Generalfeldmarschall Kesselring replaces von Rundstedt as Oberbefehlshaber West.*

12 March 1945. *Kampfgruppe Dunker attempts to defend Beckum, south-east of Münster, with four Tigers rendered immobile due to lack of fuel.*

14 March 1945. *US Army units cross the Moselle.*

15 March 1945. *Attempts by the Americans to expand the Remagen bridgehead fail. Two days later the bridge collapses.*

20 March 1945. *Saarbrücken falls to the Allies.*

21 March 1945. *Nine Jagdpanthers, the last allocated by the Heereszeugamt before the end of the war, are sent to schwere Panzerjäger-Abteilung 559.*

22 March 1945. *Hauptmann Kurt Wittmoser, the commander of 2.Kompanie, schwere Panzerjäger-Abteilung 654, is awarded the German Cross in Gold. Units of the US 3rd Army cross the Rhine at Oppenheim south of Mainz against ineffective German resistance.*

Knocked out near the Maas River crossing at Moerdijk this Jagdpanther of schwere Panzerjäger-Abteilung 559 is also shown on page 12 shortly after it was disabled. The twin driver's periscopes are clearly visible here.

23 March 1945. *Two companies of Jagdpanthers from schwere Panzerjäger-Abteilung 654, as part of Panzergruppe Hudel, attack the Remagen bridgehead. British and Canadian units begin their assault across the Rhine above the Ruhr.*

24 March 1945. *Panzergruppe Hudel's counterattack near Eitorf east of Bonn fails.*

25 March 1945. *British troops capture Wesel after an aerial bombardment almost completely destroys the town. On the following day Main and Darmstadt fall to US troops*

27 March 1945. *After fierce fighting US Army units capture Aschaffenburg.*

28 March 1945. *The Maschinenfabrik Niedersachsen-Hannover (MNH) assembly plant at Hannover is severely damaged by Allied aerial bombing effectively ending the production of new Jagdpanthers there, although existing components were utilised until 9 April when the factories were captured. British troops begin their drive towards the Elbe as the US Army captures Marburg and Limburg.*

1 April 1945. *Panzergruppe Paderborn, an ad-hoc unit scraped together from the staff of Panzer-Schule Paderborn, attacks US units at Nordborchen, north of the Dortmund to Kassel road. Two US Armies link up at Lippstadt cutting off over 300,000 German troops in the Ruhr area.*

2 April 1945. *The British 7th Armoured Division reaches the Dortmund-Ems canal and over the next week the Allies capture Recklinghausen, Fulda and Kassel and Karlsruhe on the upper Rhine.*

9 April 1945. *Kampfgruppe Schulze, with just eleven tanks, attacks the US positions near Wietersheim losing more than half its strength.*

10 April 1945. *The commander of schwere Panzerjäger-Abteilung 519 reports that all the battalion's Jagdpanthers have been destroyed.*

11 April 1945. *Tanks and infantry of Kampfgruppe Grosan, including sailors from the 2.Marine-Infanterie-Division, attack British positions at Engehausen near Buchholz where they manage to hold the enemy advance for two days. Weimar, Essen, Bochum and Goslar are captured by the Americans. The British take Celle, near Hannover, cutting the road to Hamburg. US Army units reach Schweinfurt.*

12 April 1945. *Braunschweig, the site of the Mühlenbau und Industrie AG (MIAG) factory which had produced 270 Jagdpanthers, falls to the Allies.*

13 April 1945. *Elements of Panzer-Division Clausewitz, the last German armoured division formed during the war, launch a surprise attack against British units in the area of Ülzen-Verssen, inflicting heavy casualties. The last tanks of Kampfgruppe Schulze attack a US command post at Baringhausen, west of Hannover. The US 3rd Army captures Erfurt.*

14 April 1945. *A Kampgruppe led by Oberst Erhard Grosan, the acting commander of Panzertruppenschule Bergen, attacks British units at Ahlften on the Halburger Strasse north of Soltau. Withdrawing through Bassel, one Tiger runs out of fuel and is left behind as a static defence position. On the same day, the British reach Bremen and US units capture Gera and Bayreuth.*

15 April 1945. *Arnhem is captured by the Canadians.*

16 April 1945. *The last Jagdpanther of Kampfgruppe Wiking is destroyed near Wittingen.*

17 April 1945. *British units attempt to outflank Soltau but are repulsed by the lone Tiger of Kamfgruppe Grosan left in Bassel.*

18 April 1945. *The tanks of Panzer-Division Clausewitz drive the British from their positions around Wittingen. The US Army takes Magdeburg, Düsseldorf and Nürnberg. American units advance into western Czechoslovakia. The British capture Ülzen and Lüneburg.*

19 April 1945. *With the advancing Soviet armies less than 100 kilometres to the east, the Maschinenbau und Bahnbedarf (MBA) plant at Potsdam completes a single Jagdpanther on this day. British troops launch an attack on Bremen. Leipzig and Halle fall to the Americans.*

21 April 1945. *Elements of Panzer-Division Clausewitz capture the Gifhorn-Brome road south of Wittingen, surprising US units who mistake them for Americans. French units capture Stuttgart although the Germans continue to resist around Elbingerode in the Harz Mountains.*

22 April 1945. *A total of five Jagdpanthers, probably the last vehicles produced, are assembled at Potsdam by MBA. By this time the Germans were fighting just outside the city. US 7th Army captures a bridge across the Danube. British troops reach Bremen. The next day, Dessau and Harburg are cleared of German troops and Frankfurt is captured.*

24 April 1945. *British and Canadian troops enter Bremen. US units cross the Danube at Dillingen and capture Ulm.*

25 April 1945. *US and Soviet units meet on the Elbe at Torgau south-west of Berlin.*

26 April 1945. *US troops take Regensburg on the Danube.*

28 April 1945. *The Canadians capture Emden and Wilhelmshaven, while US units take Augsburg and reach the Austrian border.*

29 April 1945. *British troops cross the Elbe near Hamburg. The US 7th Army reaches Munich.*

30 April 1945. *Hitler commits suicide appointing Grossadmiral Karl Dönitz as his successor. US and Soviet units meet at Ellenburg, south of Berlin.*

1 May 1945. *The single Tiger attached to Panzer-Division Clausewitz, which had stopped the British armoured advance near Wittingen, again manages to halt a complete tank regiment outside Schwarzenbek, east of Hamburg.*

2 May 1945. *The British reach Lübeck on the Baltic coast.*

3 May 1945. *Generalmajor Alwin Wolz, the garrison commander, declares Hamburg an open city and surrenders to the British. US troops reach the Brenner Pass on the Italian border.*

4 May 1945. *Admiral Hans-Georg von Friedeburg, representing the German government, arrives at Field Marshal Montgomery's HQ to surrender all German forces in Holland, North-west Germany and Denmark. The US 7th Army takes Innsbruck, Salzburg and Berchtesgarten.*

5 May 1945. *The US 3rd Army takes Pilsen in Czechoslovakia and prepares to drive towards Prague.*

7 May 1945. *Generaloberst Jodl as OKW Chief of Staff, signs Germany's unconditional surrender. All operations are to cease at one minute after midnight the next day.*

The MNH plant at Hannover photographed in May 1945 showing a number of Panther turrets and a single Jagdpanther. Although the photographs in this series were made in colour, attempts to identify the various coatings on the Jagdpanther must be viewed as speculative due to the amount of fire damage.

The initial organisation of a schwere Panzerjäger-Abteilung (Panther) called for a Stab, or headquarters, with three Jagdpanthers and a Stabskompanie which controlled a signals platoon (Nachrichten-Zug), an armoured engineer platoon (Pionier-Zug) and anti-aircraft platoon (Fliegerabwehr-Zug). Oberleutnant Franz Kopka, a company commander with schwere Panzerjäger-Abteilung 559, in his post-war account of the battalion's history, also mentions a medical platoon or Sanitäts-Zug. It is unlikely that all battalions had their full complement of these support units. The battalion was to contain three fighting companies, each equipped with fourteen Jagdpanthers. In early September, confirming a practice that had apparently been in place since late August, a new organisation was introduced where only the first company was to be equipped with Jagdpanthers while the second and third companies were outfitted with Sturmgeschütz III assault guns and later with Jagdpanzer IV tank destroyers. Details of these allocations are given in the text. As many German-language terms cannot be accurately translated into English I have used the originals in the diagram shown here. The expression 'frei Gliederung' refers to the concept of free organisation which was introduced in early 1944 where certain support elements, such as transport or supply, were removed from companies and held at battalion or regimental level. Kreigstärkenachweisung, abbreviated to KstN, were detailed tables of organisation issued for every unit in the army.

Two battalion command vehicles were equipped as Panzerjäger V Panther als Panzerjägerbefehlswagen with Fu8 and Fu5 radios while the third Jagdpanther had Fu7 and Fu5 sets. The Fu8 radio is easily identified by the Sternantenna aerial.

Each company commander's vehicle was equipped with an Fu8 and Fu5 radio and the four platoon commanders had Fu5 and Fu2 sets. The remaining vehicles were fitted with a single Fu5 radio.

SCHWERE PANZERJÄGER-ABTEILUNG 519

Notes

1. From late January 1944, by Hitler's order, these vehicles were renamed Nashorn, or Rhinoceros. Purely as a matter of convenience the earlier title is used in this book.

The battalion was originally formed in August 1943 and equipped with Hornisse self-propelled 8.8cm anti-tank guns (1).

Serving on the Russian front, schwere Panzerjäger-Abteilung 519 lost almost all its vehicles in the battles of June and July 1944 and was later withdrawn to Truppenübungsplatz Mielau in Germany to be rebuilt. Renamed schwere Panzerjäger-Abteilung 519 (Panther) on 15 September 1944, the battalion was organised with a Stabskompanie of three Jagdpanthers, 1.Kompanie with fourteen

Jagdpanthers and the second and third companies with fourteen Sturmgeschütz III assault guns each. On Sunday 8 October, the battalion began leaving Mielau for the front and by the following Wednesday the last train had been unloaded. The Jagdpanthers were sent into action almost immediately, supporting 1.SS-Panzerkorps and 116.Panzer-Division in the battles for the Hürtgen Forest which only ended with the commencement of Operation Wacht am Rhein, the offensive in the Ardennes.

For his actions here, particularly in the battles around the villages of Schmidt and Kommerscheidt, Hauptmann Erwin Kressmann was awarded the Ritterkreuz.

On 29 November 1944, the battalion was engaged at Lucherberg, north-west of Düren in western Germany, with seven Tiger I tanks of Panzer-Abteilung (Funklenk) 301. At this time the battalion was able to report that ten Jagdpanthers and twenty-two assault guns were available for immediate deployment. In early December the battalion was attached to 246.Volksgrenadier-Division, which had been fighting around Aachen, and by this time the first Jagdpanzer IV/70 (V) tank destroyers had arrived to supplement the assault guns. During the Ardennes Offensive the battalion was attached to 6.Panzerarmee, although it is possible that only Hauptmann Kressmann's 1.Kompanie took part in the fighting. On 7 January 1945 the battalion took part in the attempt to recapture Dahl, about 15 kilometres east of Bastogne, supporting the Führer-Begleit-Brigade and parts of 276.Volksgrenadier-Division where, despite an encouraging start, the attack was called off when ammunition supplies ran out. At the end of February the battalion was transferred to the area around Saarburg and by March was attached to a Kampgruppe commanded by Oberst Cord von Hobe. In his account of the fighting in the west during the last months of the war Edgar Christofel states clearly that from March 1945 the battalion was part of what he refers to as 'Kampfgruppe Hobe'

and took part in the fighting in the area between Ruwer and Waldrach, east of Trier (1). Other authoritative sources suggest that the remaining vehicles of schwere Panzerjäger-Abteilung 519 were under the direct control of 1.Armee from 15 March 1945, and given the fluid situation at the front, both these statements could be true.

However, the usual assumption that Kampfgruppe von Hobe is merely another name for Panzer-Brigade von Hobe is probably incorrect. Several detailed orders of battle for Panzer-Brigade von Hobe, which was originally known as Alarm-Panzer-Brigade XIII, have been published and none make any mention of either schwere Panzerjäger-Abteilung 519 or Jagdpanthers. Oberst von Hobe survived the war to serve in the Bundeswehr and his biography states that he left the Kampgruppe which bore his name in March to take up the command of 79.Volksgrenadier-Division and then Division-Bayern before leading Panzer-Kampfgruppe XIII, which is almost certainly Alarm-Panzer-Brigade XIII, in early April. This would seem to suggest that Christofel is correct and an earlier battle group commanded by Oberst von Hobe has been neglected or misinterpreted by most accounts.

In any case, by 10 April 1945, the battalion commander reported that all the unit's Jagdpanthers had been lost and the crews may have served as infantry until 5 May 1945 when the formations of 1.Armee surrendered.

Notes

1. Christofel's research was published in a two volume set entitled *Krieg am Westwall 1944/45*. It is unfortunately only available in German.

SCHWERE PANZERJÄGER-ABTEILUNG 559

Formed on Monday, 10 April 1944 at Truppenübungsplatz Mielau, the battalion's first allocation of five Jagdpanthers was made on 18 May and by the following August, the Stab and first company were fully equipped. While the battalion was still forming and completing its training, an order from Hitler directed that a new organisation be trialled with the heavy Panzerjäger units. The battalions would henceforth be made up of a single company of Jagdpanthers and two companies of Sturmgeschütz III assault guns. Schwere Panzerjäger-Abteilung 559 would be the first unit organised according to the new order, to be followed by schwere Panzerjäger-Abteilung 525 which was at that time equipped with Hornisse self-propelled guns and serving on the Italian Front (1).

The battalion was sent to the front by rail during the first week of September 1944, arriving at Tilburg in Holland, approximately 20 kilometres south-east of 's Hertogenbosch. As the Jagdpanthers were being unloaded, the commander, Major Erich Sattler, was ordered to advance towards Hechtel in Belgium to support an ad-hoc unit which was preparing to defend the town against the

advancing British. Early on Friday, 8 September Sattler's force, which included at least three Jagdpanthers, was surprised by Cromwell tanks of the Welsh Guards and Major Sattler's vehicle was quickly disabled. According to the account of Oberleutnant Franz Kopka, the commander of the battalion's 3.Kompanie, Sattler was injured so seriously when he made his escape that he was rendered unconscious for some time and although he succeeded in regaining his own lines, he was hospitalised until late November and command of the battalion temporarily passed to Oberleutnant Kopka (2).

By the end of September 1944, schwere Panzerjäger-Abteilung 559 reported that nine Jagdpanthers were on hand although just three of these were considered to be fully operational. The battalion was continuously engaged in the fighting in the Netherlands from early September until 8 December 1944, when it was withdrawn to Bullay, on the Moselle River in western Germany, and from there to Pronsfeld in preparation for Operation Wacht am Rhein, the Ardennes offensive. From 11 December 1944, the battalion was attached to Panzer-Lehr-Division,

Notes

1. The date of Monday, 11 September 1944 given for this order is problematic as it is know that the battalion had already been organised along these lines in August and was at the front before the order was issued. Just one company of schwere Panzerjäger-Abteilung 525 was transferred from Italy in 1945.

2. Sattler's Jagdpanther was recovered by the British and is today an exhibit at the Imperial War Museum.

replacing I.Abteilung, Panzer-Regiment 130 which was in Hungary. By that time, the first company, under Oberleutnant von Lengerke, was equipped with fourteen Jagdpanthers while 3.Kompanie had been issued the battalion's first fifteen Jagdpanzer IV/70 tank destroyers earlier that month. Hauptmann Honold's 2.Kompanie controlled the remaining fourteen Sturmgeschütz III assault guns.

The battalion was involved from the first day of the offensive crossing the Our River at Gemünd and Dasburg and over the next two days was with the advance units of Panzer-Lehr-Division as they captured Wiltz.

On 26 December 1944 the Panzer-Lehr-Division was replaced by 9.Panzer-Division and the second and third companies of schwere Panzerjäger-Abteilung 559 were withdrawn to St.Hubert. However, Oberleutnant von Lengerke's Jagdpanther company remained at the front and, on the same day, ran head-on into the tanks of the US 4th Armored Division near the village of Assenois as the Americans approached Bastogne from the south. Although the Germans managed to hold their positions for some time they were eventually forced to retire, ending the encirclement of Bastogne. On 28 December 1944 the battalion's second and third companies, as part of Kampfgruppe Poschinger, were fighting in the area around St.Hubert and by 30 December they had been joined by 1.Kompanie which had earlier that day beaten off an attack on Remagne, less than 10 kilometres to the south-east of St.Hubert, made by elements of US 11th Armored Division.

At this time the first company reported that just two Jagdpanthers were combat ready. In late January 1945, the battalion was supporting 79.Volksgrenadier-Division in the fighting around Krautscheid, north-west of Bitburg, and by March had been subordinated to XIII.SS-Armeekorps, which was tasked with holding the front between Stuttgart and Würzburg in western Germany.

On 20 April 1945, the battalion headquarters with one company of schwere Panzerjäger-Abteilung 559, equipped with nineteen newly-issued Jagdpanthers, was attached to 7.Panzer-Division which had been evacuated from West Prussia to Neustrelitz, north of Berlin.

Here the last Jagdpanthers of the battalion fought the Soviets until 3 May 1945 when the surviving crews gave themselves up to British units at Schwerin in northern Germany.

Photographed at Moerdijk, about 10 kilometres north of Breda, this vehicle of schwere Panzerjäger-Abteilung 559 was disabled while attempting to reach the bridge over the river Waal. The unusal insignia, just visible here on the left front fender, is reasonably clear in more than one photograph of this vehicle and a reconstructed view is shown on page 19. A later image of this same Jagdpanther is reproduced on page 7.

The Befehls Jagdpanther of Major Sattler, the battalion commander of schwere Panzerjäger-Abteilung 559, disabled near Hectel in Belgium during the first week of September 1944. The number 01, identifying the battalion commander, is clearly visible in the photograph above. This vehicle was manufactured by MIAG in July 1944 and features the single-piece gun barrel and the extra cooling pipes fitted to the left-hand side exhaust which were introduced into production from July 1944 in an effort to prevent overheating of the left engine cylinder bank. Although this Jagdpanther is fitted with the later 25mm-thick roof, it retains the larger periscope guards. This Jagdpanther is also shown and discussed further on page 19.

Photographed at some time after the end of the war, possibly as late as 1947, these three Jagdpanthers of schwere Panzerjäger-Abteilung 560 were disabled and abandoned outside the manor farm of Domaine Bütgenbach, in Belgium, during the fighting in the Ardennes. The Jagdpanthers of 1.Kompanie supported elements of 12.SS-Panzer-Division in a series of attacks here in mid-December and it appears all the battalion's losses were inflicted by towed anti-tank guns.

SCHWERE PANZERJÄGER-ABTEILUNG 560

Notes

1. A single Jagdpanther had in fact been handed over from schwere Panzerjäger -Abteilung 559 sometime in September 1944.

The battalion had served in Russia during 1943, equipped with Hornisse 8.8cm self-propelled guns, under Major Otto Streger, an experienced soldier who had been seriously wounded at Stalingrad and evacuated before the surrender. An order of 26 May 1944 directed that the battalion was to be converted to Jagdpanthers and renamed schwere Panzerjäger-Abteilung 560 (Panther).

The first allocation of Jagdpanthers did not, however, reach the battalion until October 1944 by which time it had been decided that the heavy Panzerjäger battalions in training would be equipped with a single company of Jagdpanthers and two companies of Sturmgeschütz III assault guns, or later, Jagdpanzer IV tank destroyers.

A shipment of four Jagdpanthers was despatched in October while a further ten were sent in November and early December and at the same time, the battalion was also sent eleven Jagdpanzer IV L/70 (V) (1).

The battalion took part in the Ardennes Offensive as part of Kampfgruppe Kuhlmann which was largely made up of units from 12.SS-Panzer-Division under the command of Sturmbannführer Herbert Kuhlmann. Although schwere

Panzerjäger-Abteilung 560 was probably under strength at this time, figures given in some accounts of a single Jagdpanther and four Jagdpanzer IV as combat ready are almost certainly incorrect. These numbers seem to be most frequently encountered in histories of the Hitler Jugend division and it is well known that Waffen-SS formations consistently under-reported their available armoured assets and a figure of thirteen serviceable Jagdpanthers would seem to be more realistic.

The battalion took part in the assault on Oubourcy, north-east of Bastogne, and in the fighting for control of the Büllingen to Bütgenbach road where at least three Jagdpanthers were lost.

In January 1945, the battalion was fighting in the Rhine Brückenkopf near Gambsheim and around the village of Hagenau in support of 10.SS-Panzer-Division. At this time two Jagdpanthers were allocated by the Heereszeugamt which were the first replacement vehicles the battalion had received since early December 1944.

In early February the battalion left for the east, where it remained until the end of the war fighting in Hungary and on the Oder Front.

SCHWERE PANZERJÄGER-ABTEILUNG 654

This formation was the first of the Jagdpanther battalions to be activated and the only unit to field three fully equipped Jagdpanther companies.

First formed as an independent Panzerabwehr-Abteilung in 1939 the battalion served in France and Russia and in May 1943 was the first unit to be equipped with the Ferdinand tank destroyer. On 21 February 1944, the battalion received orders to reorganise as a Jagdpanther unit but due to delays in production the first vehicles to be allocated for training were Panther tanks. The first Jagdpanthers were not issued until 23 March when five vehicles were shipped from the Heereszeugamt with a further eight received on 4 May 1944.

Although the battalion's formation progressed slowly, on 11 June 1944 Hitler ordered that the headquarters with the first and second companies must be ready to move to the Normandy Front within one week. As an interim measure the Stab would be equipped with three Panther Befehlswagen command tanks while 1.Kompanie and 2.Kompanie were expected to have twelve and thirteen Jagdpanthers respectively. This overly optimistic forecast was not met and just after midnight on 15 June 1944, 2.Kompanie left for the front with just eight vehicles. Once in Normandy the Jagdpanthers broke down almost continuously due to a variety of mechanical problems. The battalion's

first experience of combat on 11 July was also less than auspicious with one Jagdpanther hit by friendly fire and another damaged by a British anti-tank gun as it withdrew. By 6 July 1944, 3.Kompanie had managed to load their Jagdpanthers onto rail cars, with the Panthers of the battalion headquarters, but it would take eleven full days for these vehicles to arrive at the front.

Despite these early problems the Jagdpanther was able to show its power on 30 July 1944 when just three vehicles were involved in a fierce two-minute skirmish close to the village of Saint-Martin-des-Bois, south-east of Caen near Mont Pinçon, with three full squadrons of British Churchill tanks. By their own admission the British lost eleven tanks in this brief fight and later claimed to have knocked out one of the headquarters command Panthers and also damaged two Jagdpanthers, which they later found abandoned. Contradicting the British account, the Germans recorded the loss of a Befehlspanther and a single Jagdpanther and it is possible that the latter suffered some kind of mechanical fault during the battle as the crew had reported a damaged drive sprocket some days previously.

These local successes could not, however, conceal the dire supply situation in which the German units now found themselves. On 1 August 1944 the battalion was forced to write-off two Jadpanthers and by the middle of the month the unit

....text continued on page 49

Photographed in the village of Brionne during the retreat to the Seine in August 1944, both Jagdpanthers shown here are from 3.Kompanie, schwere Panzerjäger-Abteilung 654. The lead vehicle, numbered 302, is in fact towing the second Jagdpanther, the cable just visible by the left front fender. Note that the second driver's periscope has been covered by a metal plate. This battalion also added a deflector below the periscope and an angled rain guard above it.

Photographed on 13 March 1945, after the fighting for the Remagen bridgehead, this Jagdpanther is one of three vehicles lost by 1.Kompanie, schwere Panzerjäger-Abteilung 654 on that day. The battalion commonly removed all the tool racks from the hull side and the locations where they were welded to the superstructure can still be seen. The container for the gun cleaning rods was also relocated on the hull rear in the position shown here, although this example is badly damaged.

This view of the Jagdpanther depicted above shows the twin cooling pipes fitted to the left-hand exhaust and the container for the gun cleaning rods, here with the rods protruding through the open end. The field-modified stowage bin on the rear of the superstructure was an identifying feature of this battalion. This vehicle is fitted with the rear hull stowage bins with five reinforcing ribs on their outer side and although it is probably not unique, I have been unable to find another photograph of a Jagdpanther with this feature. This vehicle is also depicted on page 23 of the Camouflage and Markings section of this book.

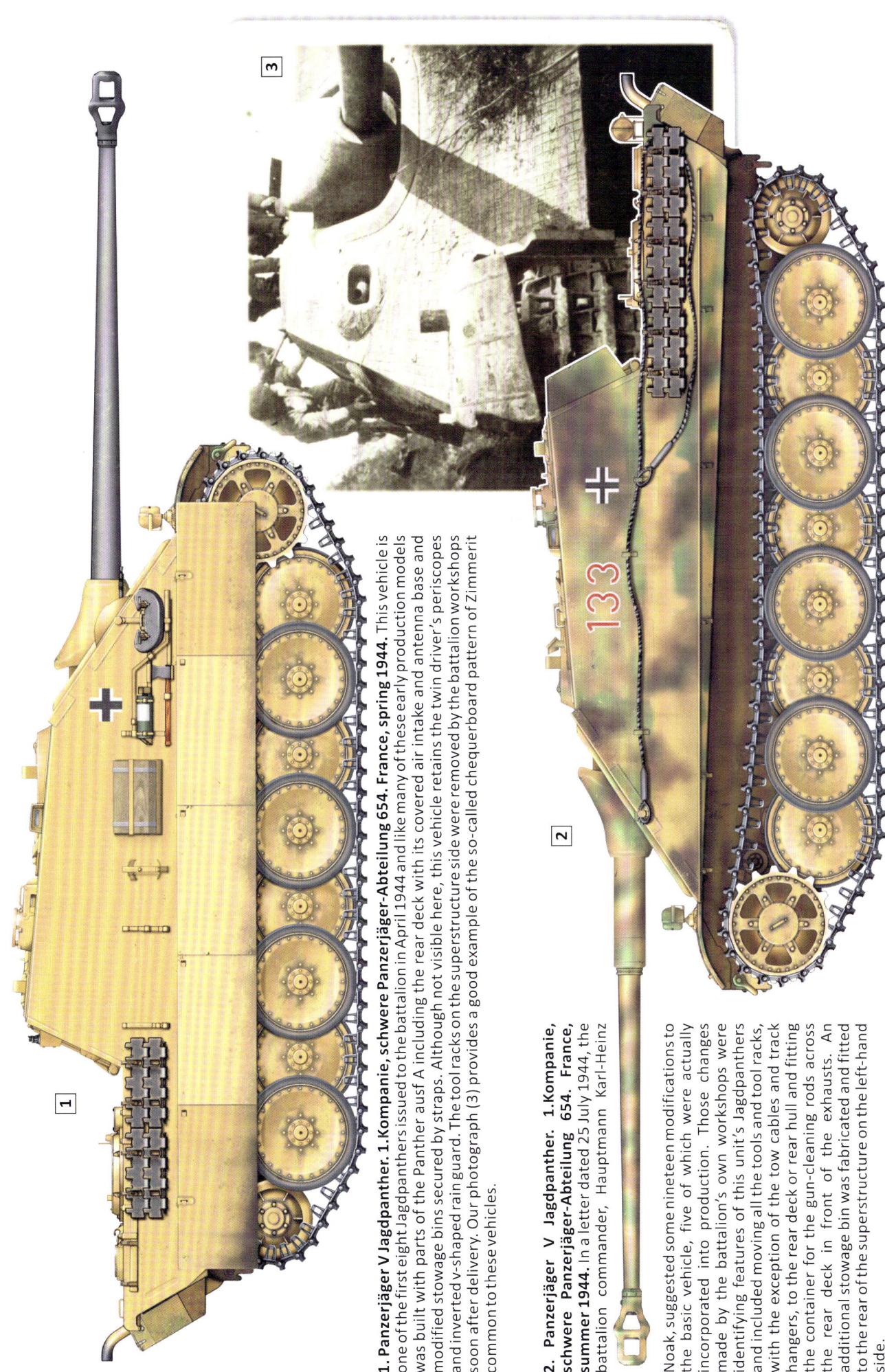

1. Panzerjäger V Jagdpanther. 1.Kompanie, schwere Panzerjäger-Abteilung 654. France, spring 1944. This vehicle is one of the first eight Jagdpanthers issued to the battalion in April 1944 and like many of these early production models was built with parts of the Panther ausf A including the rear deck with its covered air intake and antenna base and modified stowage bins secured by straps. Although not visible here, this vehicle retains the twin driver's periscopes and inverted v-shaped rain guard. The tool racks on the superstructure side were removed by the battalion workshops soon after delivery. Our photograph (3) provides a good example of the so-called chequerboard pattern of Zimmerit common to these vehicles.

2. Panzerjäger V Jagdpanther. 1.Kompanie, schwere Panzerjäger-Abteilung 654. France, summer 1944. In a letter dated 25 July 1944, the battalion commander, Hauptmann Karl-Heinz Noak, suggested some nineteen modifications to the basic vehicle, five of which were actually incorporated into production. Those changes made by the battalion's own workshops were identifying features of this unit's Jagdpanthers and included moving all the tools and tool racks, with the exception of the tow cables and track hangers, to the rear deck or rear hull and fitting the container for the gun-cleaning rods across the rear deck in front of the exhausts. An additional stowage bin was fabricated and fitted to the rear of the superstructure on the left-hand side.

1. Panzerjäger V Jagdpanther. 3.Kompanie, schwere Panzerjäger-Abteilung 654. France, summer 1944. Disabled in late July 1944, near Saint-Pierre-du-Fresne in the fighting for Hill 226, this vehicle was later recovered by the British and photographed from several angles. Like most of the battalion's Jagdpanthers this vehicle has been fitted with an additional stowage box on the superstructure rear and the tools and tool racks have been removed from the hull sides. Although the centre of the company numbers appear to be very dark in the available photographs of this battalion's vehicles, the author and historian Karlheinz Münch, in his exhaustive history of the battalion, is adamant that they were rendered in red with a white outline, as they are depicted here. The company number was usually repeated on the stowage box (3).

2. Panzerjäger V Jagdpanther. 3.Kompanie, schwere Panzerjäger-Abteilung 654. France, summer 1944. Photographed during the retreat to the River Seine in August 1944, this Jagdpanther's superstructure is covered with a large tarpaulin and at least one Zeltbahn shelter quarter. Many, but not all, the battalion's vehicles were fitted with the early monobloc single-piece gun barrel which was phased out of production from early April 1944. The soft mottled pattern of camouflage, in Olivgrün and Rotbraun on a base coat of Dunkelgelb, was commonly seen in Normandy and a series of photographs exists of a crew member from this battalion applying one of the darker shades with a spray gun. This vehicle was photographed towing another Jagdpanther of 3.Kompanie and the unit identification is based on that.

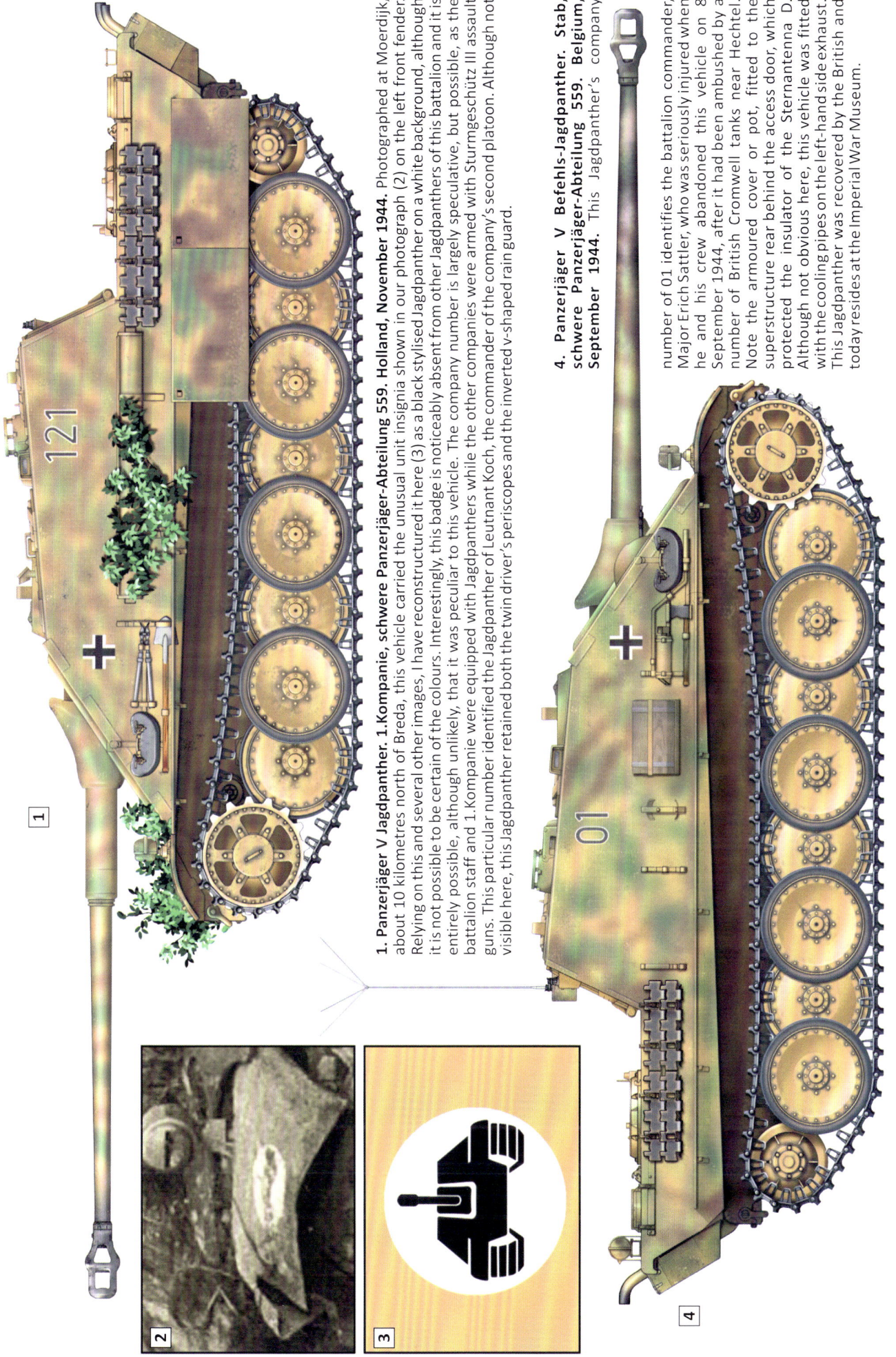

1. Panzerjäger V Jagdpanther. 1.Kompanie, schwere Panzerjäger-Abteilung 559. Holland, November 1944. Photographed at Moerdijk, about 10 kilometres north of Breda, this vehicle carried the unusual unit insignia shown in our photograph (2) on the left front fender. Relying on this and several other images, I have reconstructed it here (3) as a black stylised Jagdpanther on a white background, although it is not possible to be certain of the colours. Interestingly, this badge is noticeably absent from other Jagdpanthers of this battalion and it is entirely possible, although unlikely, that it was peculiar to this vehicle. The company number is largely speculative, but possible, as the battalion staff and 1.Kompanie were equipped with Jagdpanthers while the other companies were armed with Sturmgeschütz III assault guns. This particular number identified the Jagdpanther of Leutnant Koch, the commander of the company's second platoon. Although not visible here, this Jagdpanther retained both the twin driver's periscopes and the inverted v-shaped rain guard.

4. Panzerjäger V Befehls-Jagdpanther. Stab, schwere Panzerjäger-Abteilung 559. Belgium, September 1944. This Jagdpanther's company number of 01 identifies the battalion commander, Major Erich Sattler, who was seriously injured when he and his crew abandoned this vehicle on 8 September 1944, after it had been ambushed by a number of British Cromwell tanks near Hechtel. Note the armoured cover or pot, fitted to the superstructure rear behind the access door, which protected the insulator of the Sternantenna D. Although not obvious here, this vehicle was fitted with the cooling pipes on the left-hand side exhaust. This Jagdpanther was recovered by the British and today resides at the Imperial War Museum.

1. Panzerjäger V Jagdpanther. 1.Kompanie, schwere Panzerjäger-Abteilung 654. France, January 1945. Photographed outside Jebsheim near Colmar, this Jagdpanther may be one of the seventeen early production vehicles allocated to the battalion in July and August. It was certainly assembled before the middle of September, as evidenced by the coating of Zimmerit, and although a number of vehicles were issued in early October, the cover for the second driver's periscope, visible in our photograph, would seem to suggest that this is one of the earlier deliveries. Note that the rather rough whitewash camouflage has only been applied to the outer roadwheels.

2. Panzerjäger V Jagdpanther. 1.Kompanie, schwere Panzerjäger-Abteilung 654. France, January 1945. Photographed less than 2 kilometres from the Jagdpanther shown above, this vehicle was commanded by Unteroffizier Danisch, the leader of the first company's third platoon, and was disabled on 26 January 1945. Although this vehicle does not have the distinctive superstructure stowage box common to Jagdpanthers of this battalion, it may have been lost in combat. Note the second, much smaller Balkenkreuz just visible in our photograph (3).

1. Panzerjäger V Jagdpanther. Unidentified unit. Germany, spring 1945. Abandoned during Operation Veritable, the British crossing of the Rhine in March 1945, this Jagdpanther is a pre-September production model, indicated by the coating of Zimmerit, just visible in the original print. Other early features include the single-piece barrel of the 88mm main gun and the first type of Geschütznische, or gun recess, which was bolted internally, both of which are visible in our photograph (2).

3. Panzerjäger V Jagdpanther. 2.Kompanie, schwere Panzerjäger-Abteilung 655. Germany, spring 1945. Photographed near Kleve, on the German-Dutch frontier, this vehicle was also lost during the battles for the Rhine crossings.

From 31 October 1944, the assembly plants were advised that armoured vehicles were no longer to be painted in Dunkelgelb RAL 7028, instead they were to retain their base coat of red oxide primer to which patches of Olivgrün, Rotbraun and Dunkelgelb were to be applied sparingly. This measure was introduced in large part to counter the uneconomical use of paint by units in the field. The patterns varied considerably and that shown here seems to have been favoured, at some time at least, by MIAG. The colours of the wheels are somewhat speculative but do appear as different shades in our photograph.

1. Panzerjäger V Jagdpanther ausf G2. Unidentified unit. Germany, spring 1945. Photographed at Meppen in western Germany, approximately 5 kilometres from the Dutch border, this vehicle displays several features of late production Jagdpanthers including the raised cover for the distinctive Kampfraumheizung, or crew compartment heater, the anti-aircraft armour on the rear deck, the Flammvernichter exhaust covers and the later cast drive sprocket introduced almost at the end of the Jagdpanther's production run. Note that this vehicle is fitted with the self-cleaning rear idler, introduced into production in October 1944. These technical aspects and the introduction of the G2 version are explained in the technical section.

2. Panzerjäger V Jagdpanther. Schwere Panzerjäger-Abteilung 655. Holland, 1946. Photographed after the end of the war, perhaps as late as 1947, this vehicle appears to be an ausf G2 model with the anti-aircraft armour on the rear deck, and what may be the Kampfraumheizung, the container for the gun cleaning rods on the hull side and the later pattern Geschütznische. However, it has the early single-piece barrel (3) which was generally thought to have been phased out of production by October 1944, well before assemby of the G2 began. The many small brackets on the hull side are also unusual. Although badly worn and faded, a camouflage pattern, similar to that seen on MIAG-built vehicles, is just visible.

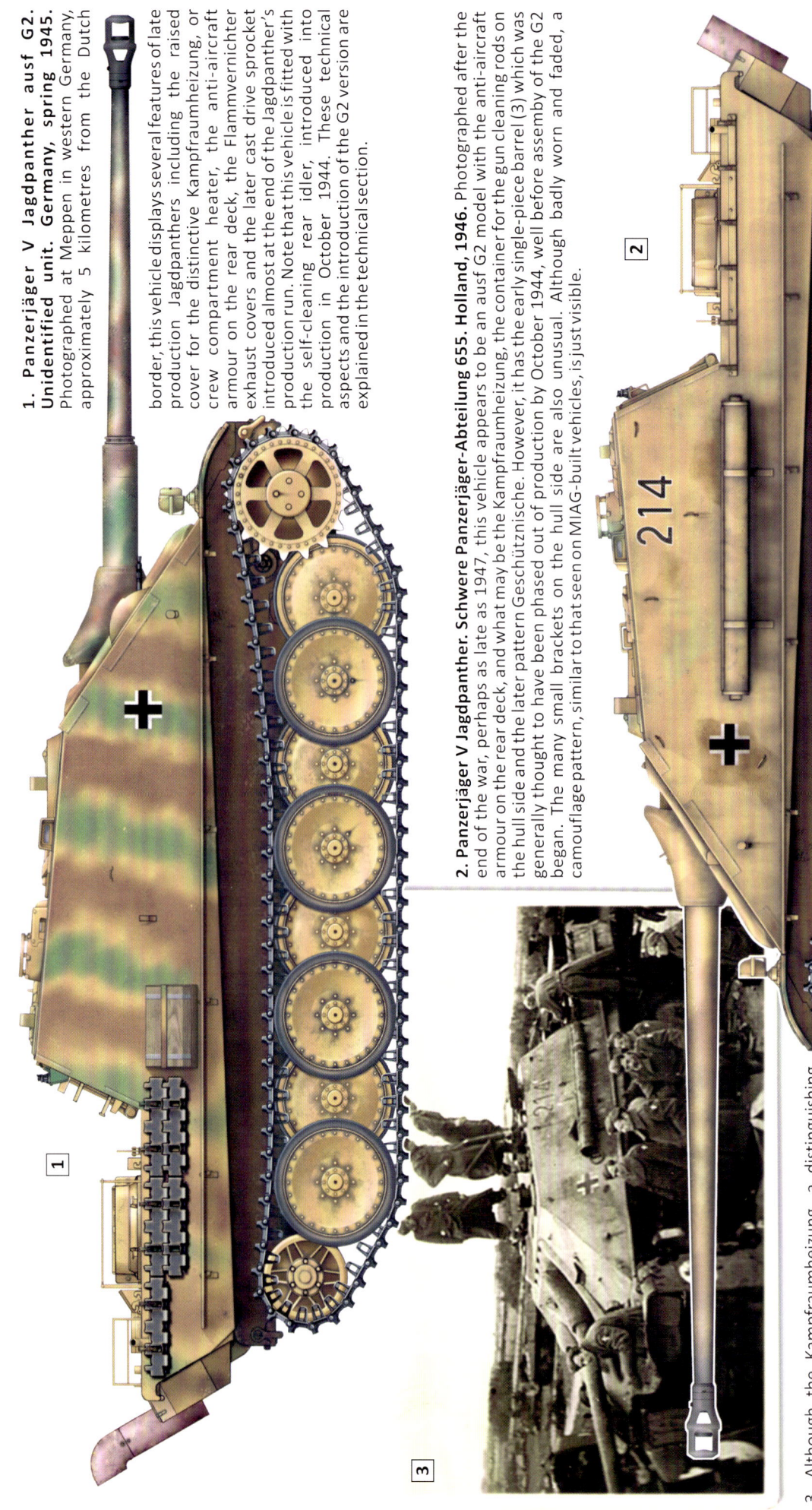

3. Although the Kampfraumheizung, a distinguishing feature of the G2, is not clearly visible here it may have been removed or, less likely, the rear deck has been taken from an early Panther ausf G with the lower-profile heater. The gun barrel is the earlier version but the Saukopfmantlet is of the type usually associated with the two-piece version and it may be that, very late in the war, some vehicles were assembled from whatever parts were available, as in fact happened with the Tiger.

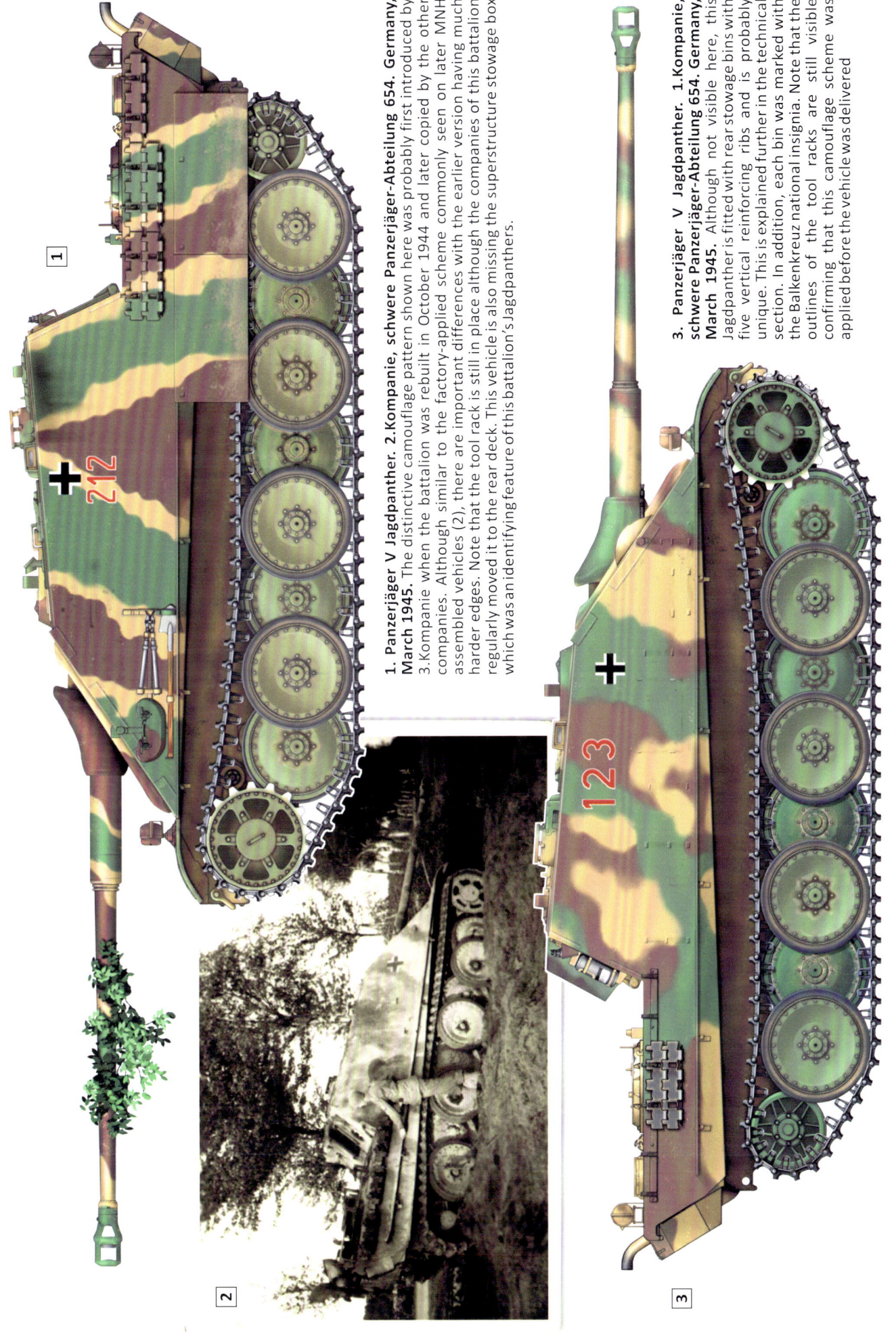

1. Panzerjäger V Jagdpanther. 2.Kompanie, schwere Panzerjäger-Abteilung 654. Germany, March 1945. The distinctive camouflage pattern shown here was probably first introduced by 3.Kompanie when the battalion was rebuilt in October 1944 and later copied by the other companies. Although similar to the factory-applied scheme commonly seen on later MNH assembled vehicles (2), there are important differences with the earlier version having much harder edges. Note that the tool rack is still in place although the companies of this battalion regularly moved it to the rear deck. This vehicle is also missing the superstructure stowage box which was an identifying feature of this battalion's Jagdpanthers.

3. Panzerjäger V Jagdpanther. 1.Kompanie, schwere Panzerjäger-Abteilung 654. Germany, March 1945. Although not visible here, this Jagdpanther is fitted with rear stowage bins with five vertical reinforcing ribs and is probably unique. This is explained further in the technical section. In addition, each bin was marked with the Balkenkreuz national insignia. Note that the outlines of the tool racks are still visible confirming that this camouflage scheme was applied before the vehicle was delivered

1. Panzerjäger V Jagdpanther. Schwere Panzerjäger-Abteilung 519. Germany, April 1945. This vehicle was photographed near Frankfurt-am-Main and the identification with schwere Panzerjäger-Abteilung 519 is based largely on that. The camouflage scheme is typical of the factory-applied patterns introduced from October 1944 and the positioning of the tool rank on the hull side indicates that this Jagdpanther was assembled by MIAG. The colours applied to the wheels are largely speculative and they may have been painted in a single shade, either Olivgrün, Rotbraun or perhaps in red oxide primer. The container for the gun cleaning rods became detached either during combat or when an attempt was made to recover the vehicle and can be seen on the ground in the photograph on which this illustration is based.

2. Panzerjäger V Jagdpanther ausf G2. II.Abteilung, Panzer-Lehr-Regiment 130. Germany, April 1945. The battalion was re-equipped with thirty-five Jagdpanther ausf G2 models, the crews collecting them from the Heereszeugamt in Braunschweig on 6 April 1945. Three vehicles were allocated to the battalion headquarters and eight to each of the four companies. All seem to have been painted in a similar camouflage scheme to that shown here, as can be seen for our photograph of a 7.Kompanie Jagdpanther (3). A short piece of coloured film, made after the German surrender, confirms that the company number was rendered in a light grey.

JAGDPANZER V JAGDPANTHER

OLDENBURG, GERMANY 1945
1/35 SCALE
GARY KWAN

Hong Kong-based modeller Gary Kwan's masterfully weathered replica is based on an MNH-produced Jagdpanther of schwere Panzerjäger-Abteilung 655 captured in the last days of the war and shown in our photograph. The methods Gary uses to achieve the worn and battered appearance are quite unique and which will hopefully be explained further in a future title.

The thorough research that Gary undertakes with each of his modelling projects is evident here and the technical details of Dragon's kit were compared with the surviving Jagdpanther at the Wehrtechnisches Museum in Koblenz, Germany, which is actually in running order.

Although most of the details incorporated into this model are covered in the Technical Details and Modifications section of this book, it is worth mentioning here the unusual flat surface of the rear stowage box which is confirmed by photographic evidence, as are the curved extensions of the Flammvernichter exhaust mufflers. The armoured covers for the air intakes and louvres of the engine deck were fabricated from pieces of hull Schürzen as an officially sanctioned field modification.

JAGDPANZER V JAGDPANTHER
EASTERN FRANCE 1944
1/35 SCALE
LIM KIAN GUAN

Lim Kian Guan's model is based on the Tamiya 1/35 Panzerjäger V Späte Version, or late model, scale kit. The amount of extra detailing is particularly impressive given that the pressure of work limits his modelling to one hour per day.

Although the kit instructions list this vehicle as unidentified, the markings are very similar to those used by schwere Panzerjäger-Abteilung 654, as depicted in our photograph.

The level of detailing and the subtle painting and weathering are shown to good effect in the images on this page. The feathered edges of the camouflage scheme are far more accurate that that suggested by the kit's manufacturer.

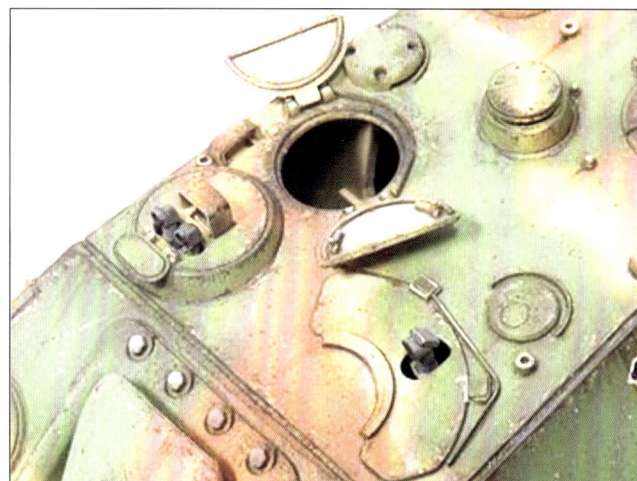

JAGDPANZER V
JAGDPANTHER
WESTERN FRONT 1945
1/48 SCALE
SEIJI IWADATE

Japanese modeller Seiji Iwadate works mostly in 1/48 scale, whenever possible with Bandai models which have been out of production for some time. His models incorporate a large amount of scratch-built detail, as can be seen in our photographs. The interior detail, shown here in the image at the top left-hand corner, is particularly impressive.

JAGDPANZER V
JAGDPANTHER

WINTER 1944-1945
1/72 SCALE
JAROSLAW WITKOWSKI

Polish modeller Jaroslaw Witkowski's Jagdpanther depicts an early production vehicle with the first pattern Geschütznische, gun recess, and single-piece barrel. Although the application of Zimmerit was discontinued from September 1944, a number of these older vehicles soldiered on until the war's end.

Jaroslaw's imposing paint job, with parts of the camouflage pattern showing through the winter whitewash, is complemented by the extremely realistic weathering to the hull and tracks. In this scale it is easy to miss the added details such as the commander's and loader's periscopes and the wood grain effect on the tool handles.

Below: Details of the rear of the superstructure, air intake grills and engine access door. The exhaust is the type introduced in July 1944, with the two extra cooling pipes fitted on the left-hand side. Note the towing cables on each side of the hull.

JAGDPANZER V JAGDPANTHER

SCHWERE PANZERJÄGER-ABTEILUNG 560
ARDENNES 1944
1/35 Scale
DU WEI JIE

Singaporean modeller Du Wei Jie's award winning model is based on the Tamiya 1/35 scale kit finished with photo-etched brass details.

The photograph at the top of the page shows Jagdpanthers of schwere Panzerjäger-Abteilung 560 disabled during the Ardennes Offensive near Büllingen.

This model includes the single length vinyl tracks and the natural sag of the full-size version has been handled particularly well here. The cloth draped across the rear deck is also a convincing, if minor, detail.

The subtle weathering of the towing clevis, tools and air intake grills can be seen here. As a late production vehicle this Jagdpanther is equipped with the 8.8cm gun with the two-piece barrel and the Geschütznische main gun recess housing incorporated into production from October 1944.

The company number and Balkankreuz are those supplied with the kit although they give the appearance of having been painted by hand. Again, contrary to the kit's instructions, the camouflage here is much closer to that applied to the actual vehicle, as can be seen from our photograph on page 34.

With its sleek lines and formidable reputation the Jagdpanther has been a favourite subject with modellers since at least the late 1960s when Tamiya released their 1/35 scale replica of this powerful tank destroyer. As impressive as this model was for its day, it was soon followed by a 1/25 scale motorised version which caused something of a sensation at the time and is still capable of fetching high prices among collectors today.

The early 1970s saw a resurgence of interest in the smaller scales, perhaps in some part due to the economic downturn, and versions of the Jagdpanther in both 1/72 and 1/76 scale were released by a number of companies which have since closed their doors including Matchbox, Nichimo, Midori and Italian manufacturer ECSI. The detailed 1/72 scale kit produced by the latter was also marketed, with little change, by Hasegawa, Polistil, Revell, Aurora and Italeri. At around this time, Bandai released their 1/48 scale kit which, although long out of production, is still popular today. It was not until 1988 that Tamiya faced any competition to its 1/35 scale model when Japanese manufacturer Gunze Sangyo released a highly detailed kit which was later the basis for DragonModel's first Jagdpanther. Until this time, Tamiya had enjoyed a virtual monopoly of the 1/35 scale market and the company responded by re-tooling some of their older products. In 2003, Tamiya began releasing a series of models in 1/48 scale, which had been largely neglected since Bandai had ceased trading, and this line has been extremely successful for the company, combining the potential for a high level of detail without the expense of the bigger kits. At the time of writing, models of the Jagdpanther are currently produced in a number of scales from tiny 6mm wargames miniatures to the large, radio-controlled 1/16 and 1/25 scale versions. Due largely to the limitations of space, however, I have chosen to concentrate here on the most popular modelling scales of 1/35, 1/48 and 1/72.

I should stress that the information presented on the following pages is far from definitive as many companies regularly withdraw products from their catalogues, often only to repackage and re-release them at some later date, and I would encourage readers to undertake their own research into the areas that interest them most. An index of manufacturers, together with suggestions for further reading, can be found on page 64 of this book. Note that although not strictly correct, I have used the terms early and late production, following the manufacturer's description.

TAMIYA INCORPORATED

Tamiya Inc. began life as a sawmill and timber supply company which also produced wooden ship and aeroplane models as a sideline. In time, these models proved so popular that the company eventually devoted itself to model making and in 1959 began working in plastic, releasing Tamiya's first model kit in 1961.

By the early 1970s, Tamiya was producing a large range of detailed armoured vehicles, together with a series of complementary figures and accessories, and was almost solely responsible for the rise in popularity of 1/35 scale, taking their lead from Airfix which had pioneered the concept of a constant scale. For their day the kits were highly detailed and accurate, but relatively easy to assemble and affordable. Tamiya's near monopoly of the 1/35 scale market remained unchallenged until the release of the first Dragon kits in 1987.

Above and at left: Tamiya's 1/48 scale Jagdpanther finished with the Eduard Model Accessories photo-etched brass detail set.

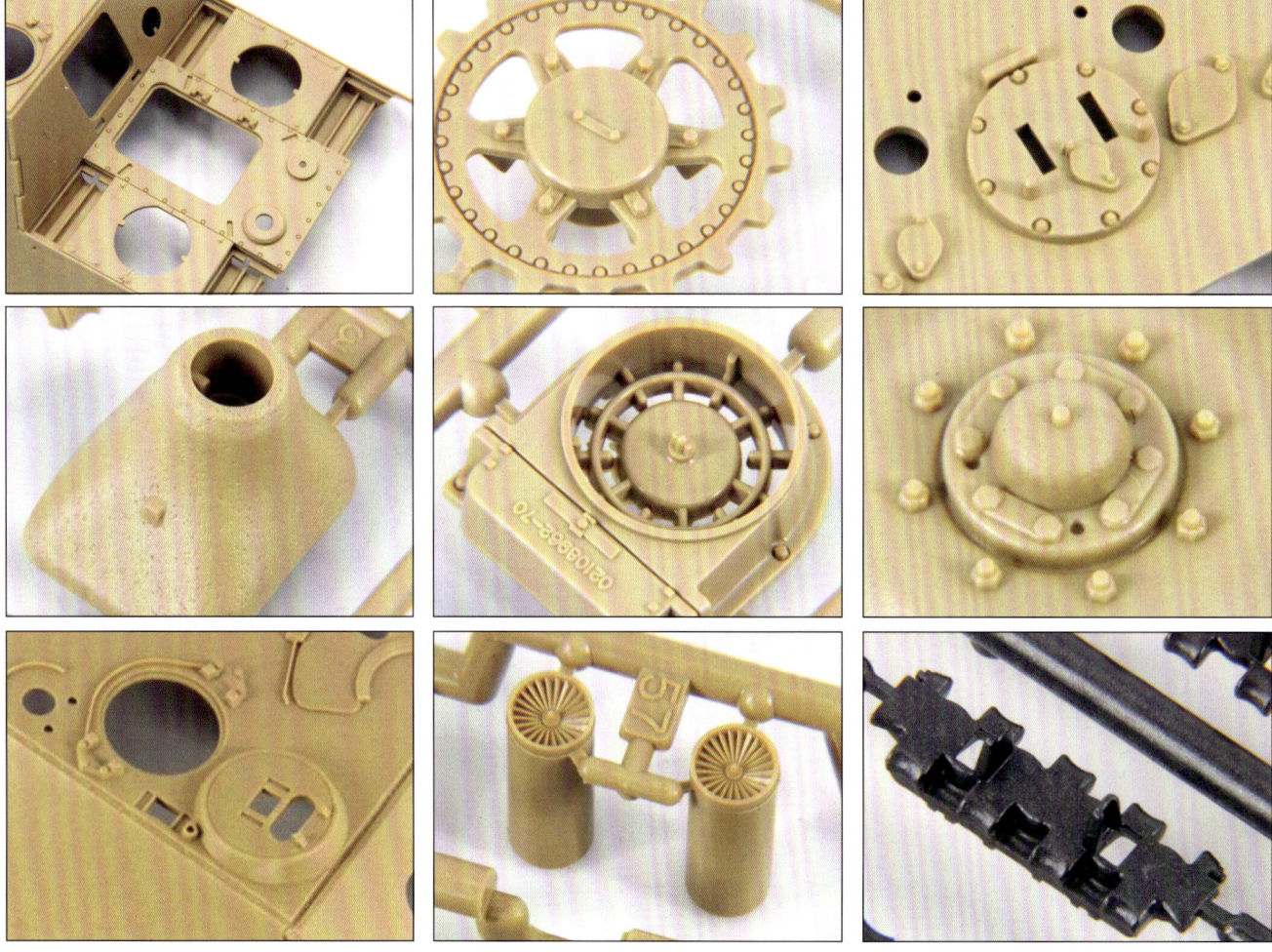

Below: Tamiya's 1/16 scale late model Jagdpanther, built straight from the box. At far right: The box art for Tamiya's 1/25 scale Jagdpanther. Originally released in 1967 this kit was re-tooled in the early 1970s. Although no longer a part of Tamiya's catalogue, it was re-released in 2010 and examples can still be found. Below: Parts from Tamiya's 1/35 scale late production Jagdpanther. First released in the late 1960s, this kit received a major overhaul in 1996.

At the time of writing Tamiya produces 1/16 scale replicas of the Jagdpanther, in both static and motorised versions, early and late production variants in 1/35 scale and a late production 1/48 scale model. Although the 1/25 scale offerings are no longer included in the company's catalogue they are still listed as available from a number of major retailers and have in any case been re-released by other manufactures as will be explained later. In addition, the company produces a number of accessories such as detailed track sets made up of individual links and ammunition for the 88mm gun.

DRAGON MODELS LTD

This Hong-Kong based company's reputation for detail and accuracy is well deserved. At the time of writing Dragon offered six construction kits in both 1/35 and 1/72 scale, representing early production Jagdpanthers, both with and without Zimmerit, a late production model and also a kit marketed as the G2 version. Although the first of the 1/35 scale models was released in 1995, all have been upgraded since then, some with additional parts

The first small scale kit was released in 2003 and was far superior to any similar models then available. In addition to the construction kits Dragon produces a number of assembled and pre-painted display models in 1/72 scale which are essentially the same as the smaller scale models. These come in a variety of markings and depict vehicles in service from the battles in Normandy until the last weeks of the war in 1945.

Above: Dragon's early Jagdpanther in 1/35 scale, first released in 1995 and re-tooled in 2007 and 2009. At right: One of the pre-painted display models in 1/72 scale display models. Below: The Jagdpanther G2 kit built with additions from Eduard Model Accessories.

Below: Dragon's early Jagdpanther with Zimmerit in 1/35 scale built straight from the box. In addition to the photo-etched details shown here the kit contains clear plastic parts and a metal towing cable.

EDUARD MODEL ACCESSORIES

Founded in 1989 by two enterprising modellers, this Czech company produces high quality photo-etched brass detail sets and a number of scale models. The sets vary in size and price from basic details such as fenders to complete updates for a particular vehicle. Currently available are extensive photo-etched sets to update the Jagdpanther G2 from Dragon with a set containing the necessary parts to build a Panzerbefehlswagen including a Sternantenna D.

There are also sets for both the Italeri and Tamiya 1/35 scale models and for the the Tamiya 1/48 scale late production Jagdpanther. Examples of these are shown below. Eduard also produces vinyl masks to assist with painting the Jagdpanther road wheels in both 1/48 and 1/35 scale. Unfortunately, the photo-etched set for the Dragon 1/72 scale kit is currently unavailable, although this may be re-released at some later date.

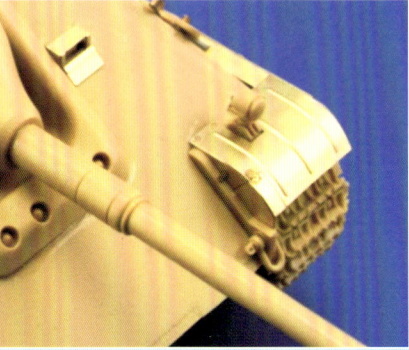
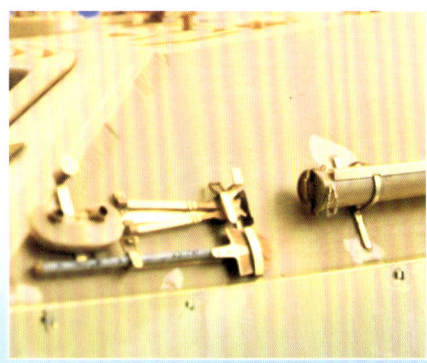

Above: The photo-etched detail set produced for the Tamiya 1/48 scale late production Jagdpanther.
Below: The Dragon Models Jagdpanther G2 built with Eduard's photo-teched detail set. Upgrades to replace the rear stowage boxes are also available.

Below: The Dragon Models 1/72 scale early Jagdpanther with Zimmerit built with Eduard's photo-etched detail set. Although this set is listed as discontinued it is still available from some major retailers.

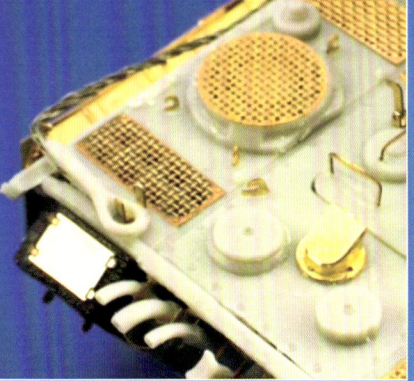

ACADEMY

Based in Korea this company produces an extensive range of 1/35 scale figures and vehicles as part of its Military Miniatures range. Although the company claims that the Jagdpanther is a completely new kit, its resemblance to the old Tamiya 1/25 scale model, even unassembled, is quite obvious. I have been assured by a reliable source that a number of the Academy motorised kits also included the figures that accompanied the Tamiya model and that the Tamiya tracks, which are still available, will fit the Academy kit including the motorised version. As an Academy release, this model has gone through at least four re-boxings, two of which are shown here. As with the Tamiya kit, the motorised version has individual track links while the static model comes with single length vinyl tracks.

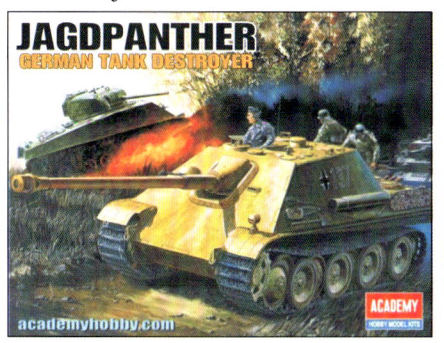

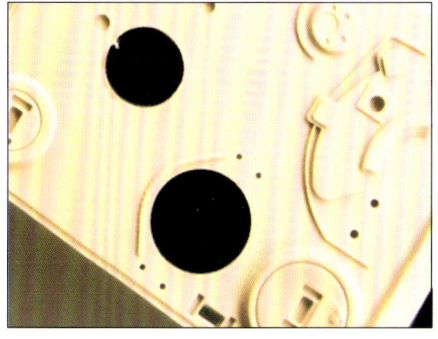

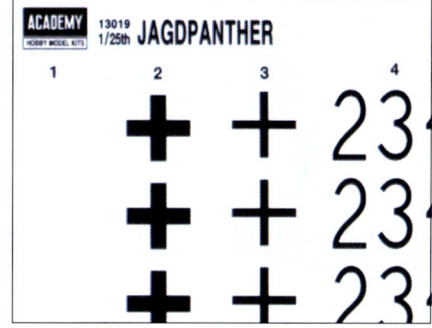

ITALERI

This Italian company has been producing plastic models since its foundation in 1962. The company's 1/35 scale Jagdpanther was first released in 1994, with a re-boxed version offered in 2007, and although a basic kit by today's standards, it is accurate and easy to assemble and its budget price will appeal to many modellers. In 2015, the Italeri kit was released in eastern Europe under Zvezda's logo with no change except the choice of markings and the colour of the plastic. Italeri's 1/72 scale Jagdpanther is a re-boxing of the ESCI kit which was first released in the late 1960s and re-tooled in 1975. In 1987, this kit, with most of ESCI's armour models, was marketed with hard plastic link and length tracks which was something of an innovation at the time.

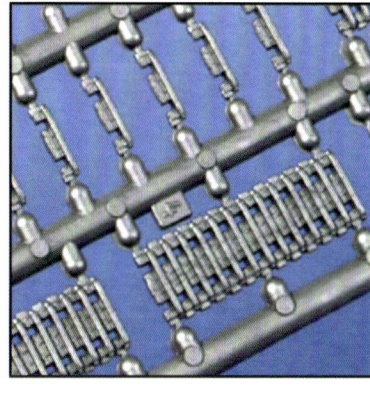

At far left: Italeri's 1/72 scale Jagdpanther. The box art for the 1/35 scale kit is almost identical. At left: The Italeri/ESCI 1/72 scale model detailed and painted by Polish modeller Jaroslaw Witkowski. Besides the anti-aircraft shields on the air intakes and the infrared night sight, many small details have been added. Above: Parts for the Italeri 1/72 scale kit including the hard plastic link and length tracks.

REVELL

This company offers a number of Jagdpanther kits in both 1/35 and 1/72 scale and most are re-boxings of older kits. The 1/35 scale Early Jagdpanther is in fact the Dragon Command Version kit which was upgraded in 1995 with the addition of new parts. This model features the single-piece 88mm gun barrel. Dragon later re-released this kit in 2004 as a Jagdpanther Early Version. Revell's Late or Command version was again based on the Dragon model and the only difference seems to be the box art and the inclusion of the two-piece barrel. It appears that at least one of the smaller scale Jagdpanthers, although initially marketed as 1/72 scale, is the old 1/76 scale Matchbox kit which would at least explain the often heard criticisms regarding the model's dimensions. The 1/72 sale Jagdpanther released in 1997 is based on Revell's Panther ausf G with the same wheels, lower hull and tracks. Although not equal to the later Dragon releases, this is an accurate model.

At right: Revell's Jagdpanther kit based on the company's Panther ausf G with the hard plastic tracks that are included in the kit.

The 1/72 scale Jagdpanther kit built and painted by the author.

GPM MODELE KARTONOWE

This Polish company produces a large range of model kits made from heavy-weight paper and wood which arc surprisingly dctailcd considering the medium. In addition to aircraft, ships, architectural subjects and figures, GPM offers a number of armoured vehicles in different scales. The company also manufactures a variety of tracks, gun barrels and ammunition madc from wood. Pictured below are images of the company's 1/25 scale Jagdpanther which incorporates extensive interior detailing.

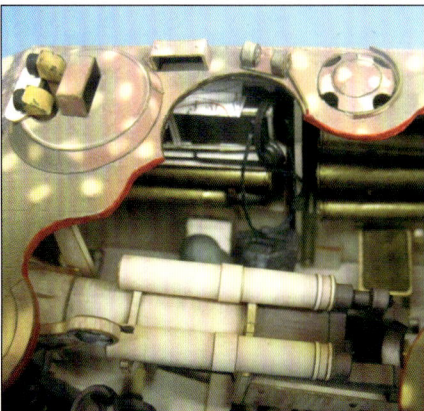

EDUARD MODEL ACCESSORIES

Founded in 1995, this Polish company has been manufacturing and selling high quality upgrade sets, produced in photo-etched brass, milled aluminium and brass, stainless steel and even wood. The company produces detail sets and accessories in 1/16, 1/25, 1/35 and 1/48 scale. In addition they offer highly-detailed barrels and muzzle brakes for the 88mm gun in the same scales. Although many of the sets are listed as discontinued they are still available from major retailers.

Shown below are details fitted to the Tamiya 1/48 scale kit at 1 and 2, the Dragon early production version at 3 and 4 and the Dragon late model at 5 and 6. Many of the items listed as appropriate for the Panther ausf G could also be used for the Jagdpanther and a number of generic items, such as radio antenna insulators, would also be correct.

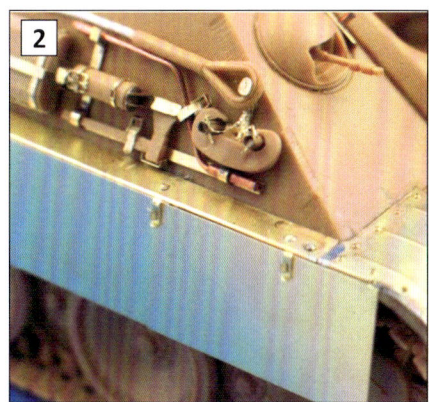

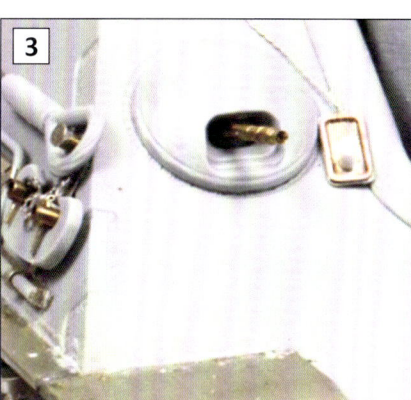

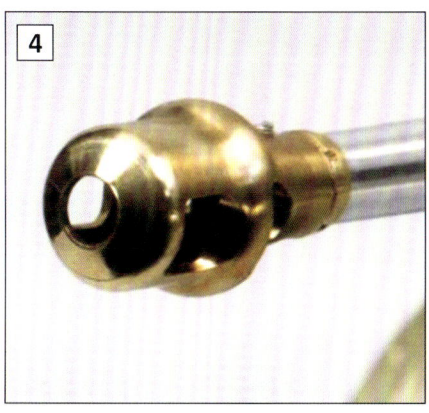

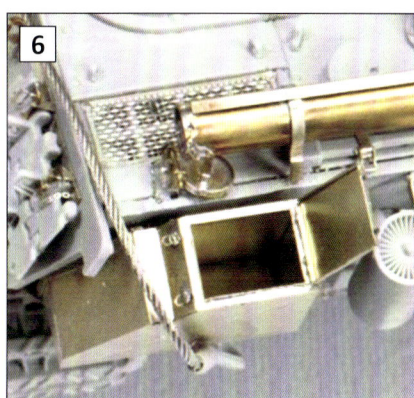

VOYAGER MODEL

Voyager have been manufacturing upgrade sets for scale models since 2003 with the release of their first products chiefly aimed at 1/35 scale armour modellers. The company also produces turned aluminium barrels for both the late and early 88mm guns of the Jagdpanther in 1/35 scale. Shown here in the main picture is the complete upgrade set for the late production Dragon kit which includes damaged road wheels in resin. Below that, from left to right, parts of the detail set in 1/35 scale for an early production model, the container for the gun cleaning rods, also in 1/35 scale, and the Dragon Models 1/72 scale Jagdpanther built with Voyager's photo-etched brass details.

RB MODEL

RB Model from Poland produce a range of highly detailed milled aluminium and brass gun barrels and resin accessories in various scales. Shown here, from left to right, are the 88mm KwK 43/3 L/71gun with the early type muzzle brake, the same gun with the later-style muzzle brake, both in 1/48 scale, and the 1/72 scale 88mm KwK 43 L/71. The company also produces appropriate ammunition in brass.

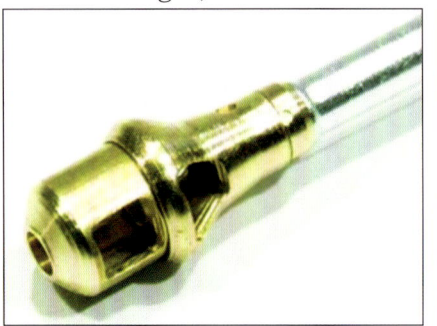

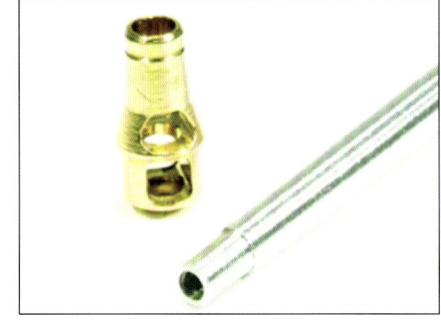

MODEL ARTISAN MORI

This small Japanese company produces resin upgrade parts for 1/35 scale armour models including a number specifically created for the Panther and Jagdpanther as well as more generic items such as fire extinguishers, tow shackles and bolt cutters, a 20-ton jack and Bosch headlights. Sadly, the range of excellent Panzer crew figures is no longer available.

Above, from left to right: Resin details in 1/35 scale from Model Artisan Mori. Replacement drive sprocket, stowage box for infrared sighting-equipped vehicles and discarded Panzer jackets.

ALLIANCE MODEL WORKS

Although a relative newcomer this US-based company boasts an extensive catalogue which includes large conversion sets and upgrades in resin, photo-etched brass and machined metals for military vehicles, combat aircraft, ships and fantasy/science-fiction subjects. In addition Alliance also offer a range of water-slide transfers and airbrush masks. The armour products are mostly restricted to 1/35 scale, although there are a number of photo-etched brass sets of uniform details for 1/16 scale crew figures. The complete set for the Dragon Jagdpanther is shown below and other smaller sets are available for items such as the air intake grills and all are reasonably priced.

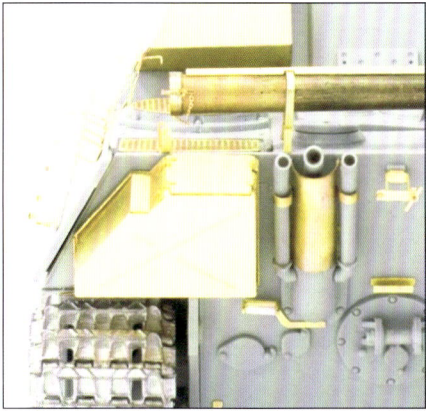  

ROYAL MODEL

This Italian company has been producing high quality accessories and after market parts since the early 1990s under the guidance of its founder, Roberto Reale.

The catalogue includes complete upgrade sets in 1/35 scale for the early and late production Jagdpanther and although these are specifically marketed for the Italeri and Tamiya kits, most of the parts would be suitable for the scale models of other manufacturers. In addition to the accessory sets, Royal Model also offer a number of detailed Panzer crew figures in a variety of uniform styles in 1/35 scale. More generic parts in resin and brass include a Panther engine transmission, detailed rear stowage bins, engine grills and a Kugelblende machine gun mount. Royal Model also market a limited number of sets in 1/72 and 1/48 scale and crew figures for the larger scale models.

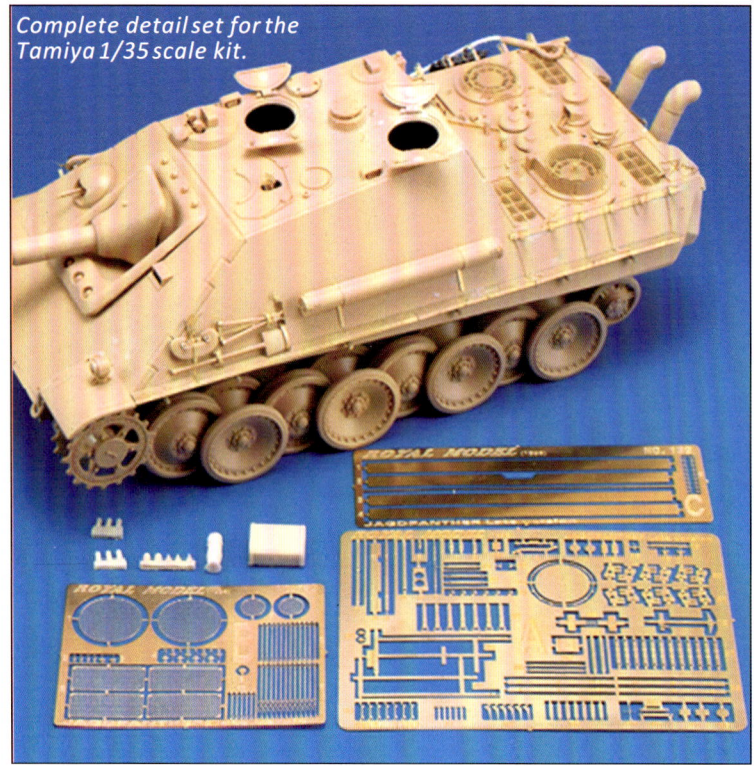

Complete detail set for the Tamiya 1/35 scale kit.

Photo-etched air intake grills and later style exhaust shrouds in resin.

Panther and Jagdpanther transmission in 1/35 scale.

E.T. MODEL

E.T. Model, a relatively new manufacturer from China, produces detailed upgrade sets in 1/72 and 1/35 scale in brass and resin. Although their catalogue is extensive, the company's single offering for the Jagdpanther is produced specifically for the 1/72 scale Dragon kit, which is shown below, but could probably be used with the Revell or Italeri models. Most detail sets are specifically designed, according to the company, to fit Dragon or Tamiya kits but some are referred to as universal. It is possible that E.T. Model had ceased trading just prior to the time of writing, however, as I have been unable to obtain a definite answer from the company, I have decided to include it here.

GRIFFON MODEL

Based in China this company produces a large range of accessories and upgrade sets in photo-etched aluminium, resin and styrene in 1/35, 1/72 and 1/144 scale. The range covers not only armoured vehicles but also artillery pieces and ships. Shown below are: 1 to 3. The Late Production Premier Edition complete upgrade in 1/35 scale.

4. Parts of the Command Version set including a resin antenna insulator and armoured cover. 5. Vehicle tool set in 1/35 scale. 6. Upgrade set for the Dragon 1/35 scale Early Production model. This company should not be confused with Griffon of Japan or Griffon Model Accessories from Poland, which produce aftermarket items for aircraft.

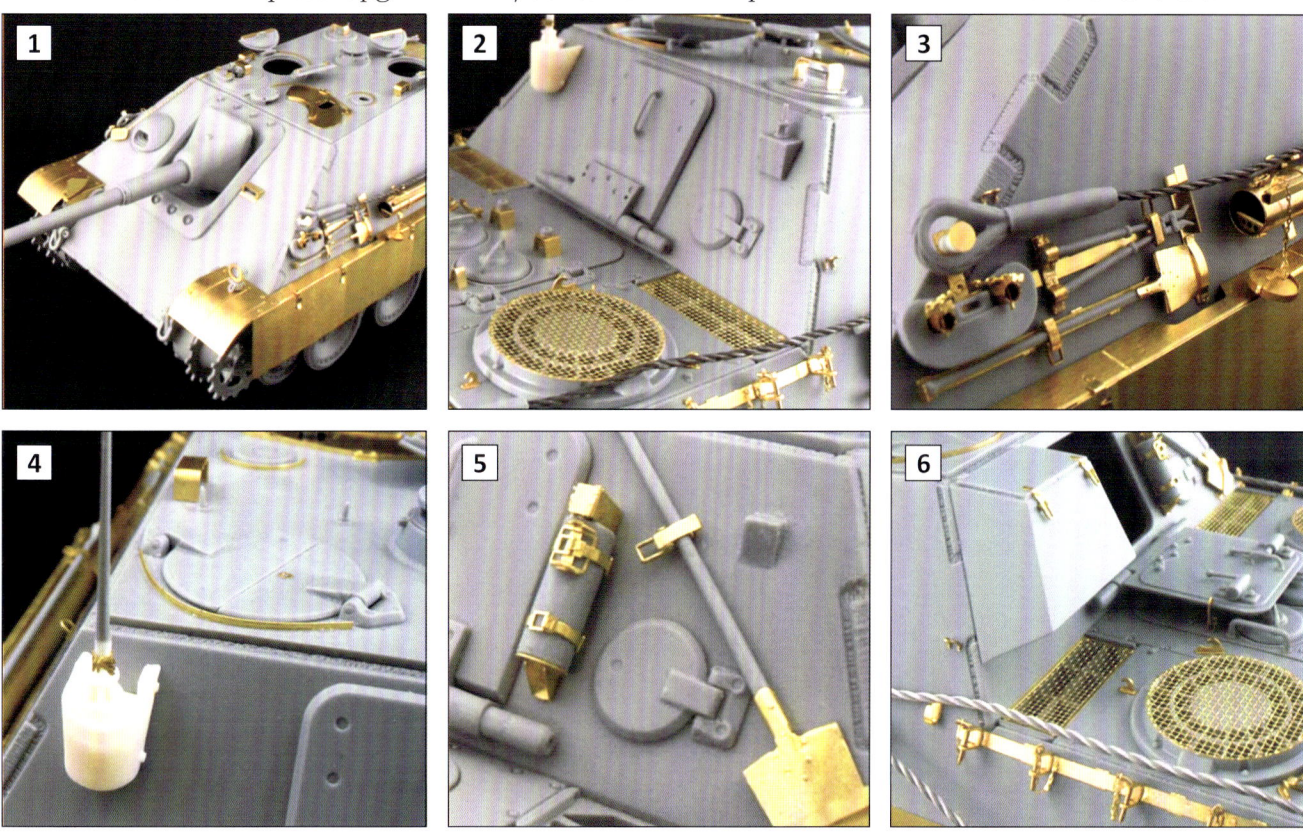

HAULER

Based in the Czech Republic, this company produces accessory sets in photo-etched brass and resin in 1/48, 1/35 and even 1/87 scale. A number of products are also marketed under the Brengun logo. Hauler's current catalogue contains upgrade sets for the Armourfast 1/72 scale Jadgpanther as well as the Tamiya 1/48 scale model, shown below, and a generic 1/87 scale set.

BLACK DOG

Based in the Czech Republic this company produces a large range of detailed resin accessory and upgrade sets for armoured vehicles in 1/35, 1/48 and 1/72 scale and a small number of complete kits. Products specifically marketed for the Jagdpanther are, however, quite limited but interesting as they all depict damaged parts and equipment. From left to right, Panther and Jagdpanther road wheels, a gun cleaning rod container and a set of rear stowage boxes.

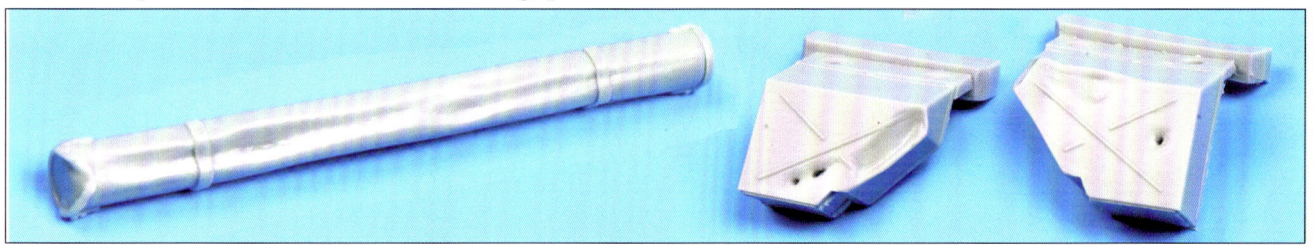

AFTERMARKET TRACKS

Most plastic kits today contain realistic tracks made from a form of vinyl which, unlike the older types, can be glued together or hard plastic individual links. Nevertheless, there are many modellers who wish for the highest level of detail and realism possible and consequently the number of quality aftermarket products available seems to have increased in recent years, despite the extra expense and work required. In order to operate properly, motorised models require workable tracks made up from individual links held together by pins, as were the full size items.

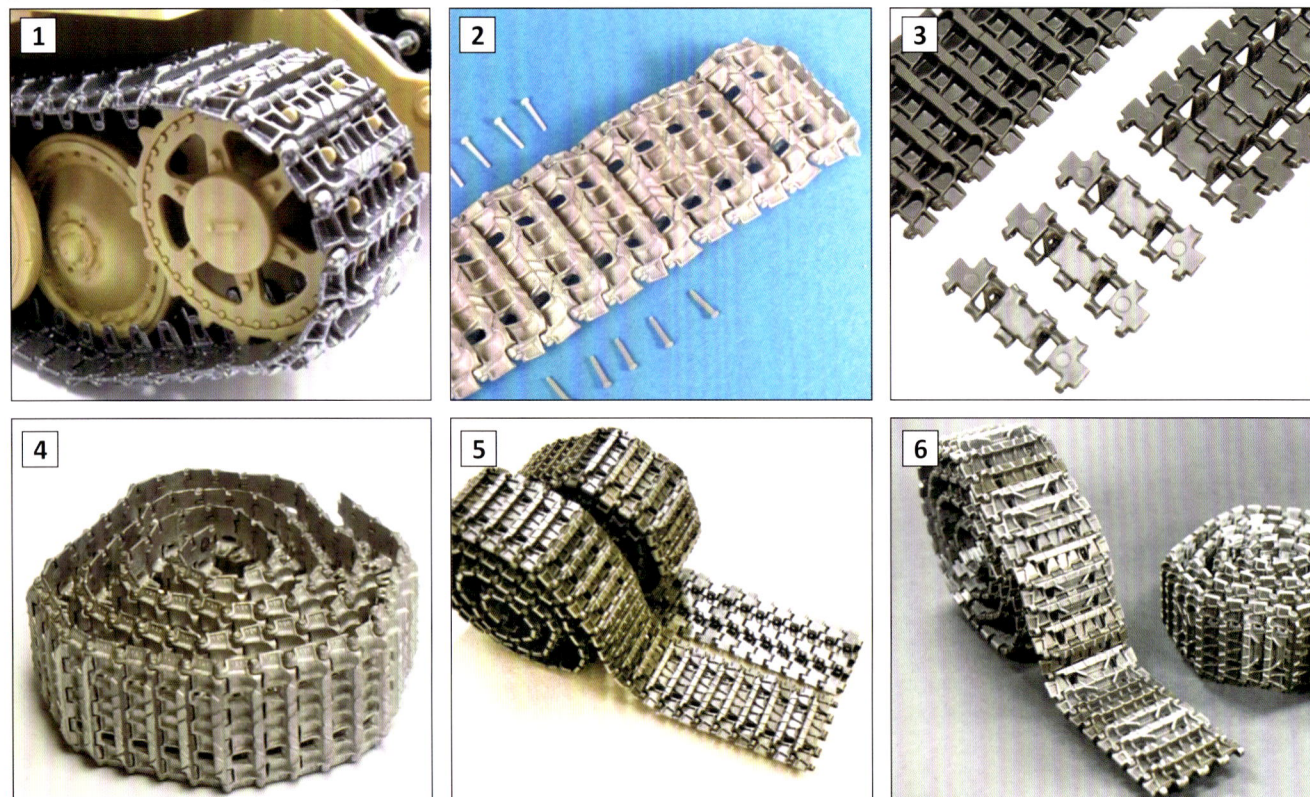

:Above: 1. Kaizen plastic 1/35 scale Panther and Jagdpanther late type Kgs 64/660/150 workable tracks available from MS Models, Japan. 2. MasterClub 1/35 scale late Panther tracks. This is a relatively new company from Russia fast gaining a reputation for detail and accuracy. 3. Tamiya's 1/35 scale workable Panther tracks in plastic. 4. Friulmodel metal 1/35 scale late model Panther tracks. 5. DKLM RC 1/16 scale tracks for the Tamiya motorised kit. 6. Taigen 1/16 scale workable metal tracks.

MARKINGS

Unlike many of the tanks covered in previous volumes of this series, the Jagdpanther is not particularly well cater for with aftermarket waterslide transfers, or decals to our American readers. Most of the markings offered for the larger scale models cover the vehicles of schwere Panzerjäger-Abteilung 654 during its service in Normandy or depict what are really generic insignia such as various styles of company number or different sizes of Balkenkreuz. This does reflect the historical record to some extent as, by the late war period, it is common to see photographs of Jagdpanthers with no markings at all. However, some companies do often some rather pleasing options, the most extensive, rather unusually, in 1/87 scale.

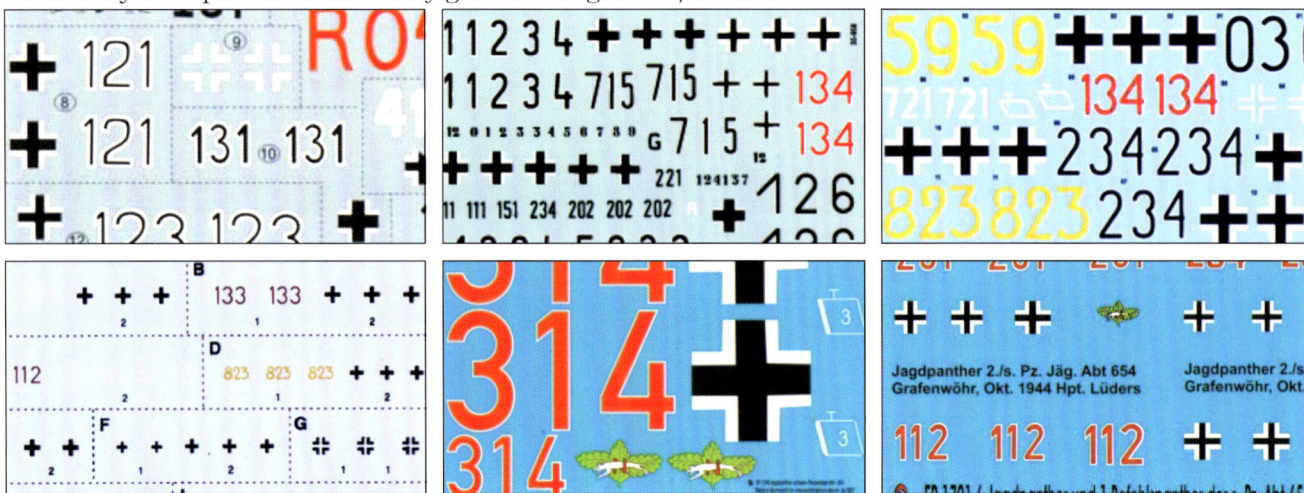

Above: 1. Part of the Armo 1/35 scale sheet. 2. Star Decals in 1/35 scale. 3. Elite Armor's 1/16 offering. 4. Komo from Fidelis Models markings for 1/87 scale Jagdpanthers. 5. Peddinghaus, also in 1/87 scale. 6. Peddinghaus transfers for a 1/16 scale model.

Photographed in February 1945 near Hettenschlag, 10 kilometres south-east of Colmar, this Flakpanzer IV Wirbelwind is one of four such vehicles received by schwere Panzerjäger-Abteilung 654 in October 1944.

Continued from page 15...

strength dropped from twelve operational Jagdpanthers to just one.

On 3 August, 1.Kompanie was declared combat ready, despite having just eight Jagdpanthers, and was ordered to Normandy. Travelling by rail as far as Chalons, and continuing from there on their own tracks, the company reached the front on 16 August 1944 as the German army in the west was in retreat. In the withdrawal to the Seine the battalion lost a total of nineteen Jagdpanthers in defensive actions but they managed to cross the river with twenty-eight serviceable vehicles which was quite an achievement given the chaos that prevailed.

The battalion was withdrawn from the front line on 9 September 1944 and sent to Grafenwöhr in Germany to refit where it was found that a number of the Jagdpanthers were so badly worn that they required complete replacement engines. During October and early November the battalion was rebuilt to an authorised strength of forty-five Jagdpanthers and in addition received a Fliegerabwehr-Zug, made up of four Flakpanzer IV armed with 3.7cm guns and a further four with 2cm quadruple mountings, and four Bergepanther recovery vehicles. On 18 November, the battalion began moving back to the Western Front.

Attached to LXIII.Armeekorps, the battalion was continuously in action during the last weeks of November and claimed fifty-two enemy tanks and ten anti-tank guns destroyed while a further nine Allied tanks were damaged. The battalion's own losses were, however, significant, accounting for eighteen Jagdpanthers and three of the Flakpanzers.

During late November, Schwere Panzerjäger-Abteilung 654, with a total operational strength of twenty-three Jagdpanthers, was split into four Kampfgruppen named Blasius, Lüders, Schnepf and Wittmoser (1). These battle groups were named for the commanders of the first, second, third and headquarters companies respectively. The practice of attaching individual companies to other formations continued until the end of the war and a further battle group, Kampfgruppe Schmidt, was formed in early January 1945 and probably replaced the second company Kampfgruppe when Hauptmann Friedrich Lüders was wounded.

For the planned offensive in the Ardennes, Oberkommando des Heeres proposed that five heavy Panzerjäger formations would take part, fully equipped with Jagdpanthers and assault guns or tank destroyers. However, of these five battalions, three had been at the front for some time and were well below their authorised strength. Schwere Panzerjäger-Abteilung 654 did not participate in the attack, remaining on the southern edge of the front under the

Notes

1. The figure reported for 1 December 1944 was twenty-five and the two additional Jagdpanthers may have been the vehicles whose railway car was forced to fall out when the battalion returned to the front in mid-November.

Notes

1. Accounts of these last battles are understandably confused and it is possible that some individual Jagdpanthers fought on elsewhere.

command of Oberkommando Oberrhein reporting that twenty-six Jagdpanthers were on hand on 16 December 1944. On Christmas Day the battalion received ten replacements and a further nine on 5 January 1945.

During the first weeks of January 1945, as part of Operation Nordwind, the battalion supported Panzer-Brigade 106 Feldherrnhalle in an attack in the Wittisheim area to secure the Rhein-Rhône canal and at the end of the month took part in the assault on Jebsheim in the Colmar Pocket. In February 1945, 1.Kompanie of schwere Panzerjäger-Abteilung 525 was attached to the battalion as a fourth company and received six Jagdpanthers that arrived on 7 March 1945. During that month, as part

of Kampfgruppe Hudel, elements of the battalion took part in the fighting for the Remagen bridgehead while a Kampfgruppe under Oberleutnant Waldemar Paffrath, the fourth company commander, was tasked with securing the area around Fernegierscheid.

On 28 March 1945, two Jagdpanthers, the survivors of Oberleutnant Wolf's and Oberleutnant Paffrath's Kampfgruppen, were ordered to Roth, east of Seigburg, and later that day to Bitzen which they managed to reach with the last of their fuel and these may have been the battalion's last serviceable vehicles (1).

On 15 April 1945 the survivors of schwere Panzerjäger-Abteilung 654 surrendered to the Americans.

A Jagdpanther ausf G2 of schwere Panzerjäger-Abteilung 654 photographed near Düren in western Germany on 15 March 1945. Note the armoured guards for the roof periscopes which are the smaller, 100mm high versions and the simplified Kugelblende machine gun mount which was the last model introduced into production. Also note the Balkenkreuz national insignia on the glacis below the main gun. As early as 11 December 1944 the battalion commander, Hauptmann Karl-HienzNoak, reported that the frontal armour of the Jagdpanther was no longer able to resist the power of the new Allied tank and anti-tank guns.

SCHWERE PANZERJÄGER-ABTEILUNG 655

The battalion had served on the Russian Front until 13 September 1944 when it was reorganized at Truppenübungsplatz Mielau in Germany as a schwere Panzerjäger-Abteilung (Panther). Although some sources state that the third company remained in Russia, I have not been able to confirm this and it is certain that the battalion was made up of three full companies at Mielau.

The first five Jagdpanthers were shipped from the Heereszeugamt on 24 November 1944 and these were allocated to 2.Kompanie. On the following day twenty-eight Jagdpaner IV/70 (A) tank destroyers were despatched for the first and third companies and in early December a further three were allocated to the battalion headquarters.

During the first week of December 1944, the first and third companies left for the front while the second company remained at Mielau, waiting for their last delivery of Jadgpanthers which were not shipped until Christmas Eve. On 15 January 1945 the first of the battalion's Jagdpanthers arrived at the front and took part in the fighting in the Reichswald.

At some time in early 1945, or possibly late 1944, the battalion's 3.Kompanie was removed and renamed schwere Panzerjäger-Kompanie 669. Equipped with Hornisse self-propelled anti-tank guns, the company was sent to the east.

From the beginning of March 1945 the battalion was attached to Korps-Bayerlein, part of 15.Armee holding the front north of Koblenz (1).

On 5 April 1945, the battalion was withdrawn from the front line and sent to Sulingen, south of Bremen, to rest and re-equip. At this time 2.Kompanie reported that eight Jagdpanthers were on hand although how many of these were completely serviceable is not known. On 7 April the battalion was assigned to 12.Armee and two days later was informed that ten Jagdpanthers and a Bergepanther, with their crews and full ammunition supplies, were in transit from Braunschweig. In addition, a prototype Jagdpanther that was found at the MIAG factory was promised to the battalion.

Under the command of General Walther Wenck, 12.Armee was ordered to break through the Soviet encirclement of Berlin and managed to reach Potsdam before Wenck realised he could go no further. He did, however, manage to keep an escape corridor open to Tangermünde and the Elbe crossing.

It is unknown if any of the Jagdpanthers took part in these actions and the battalion surrendered to the Canadians in early May near Oldenburg, north-west of Bremen, close to the positions they occupied at the beginning of April.

Notes

1. Also referred to in some accounts as Division-Bayerlein, this formation was built around the last units of LIII.Armeekorps. The name I have used here is that noted on the OKW situation map for 21 March 1945.

Photographed near Cleve in February 1945 this Jagdpanther of 2.Kompanie, schwere Panzerjager-Abteilung 655 is an MNH-manufactured vehicle identified by the ventilator in the centre of the roof near the front which was indicative of Jadgpanthers produced in November and December 1944. This vehicle has a number of metal loops welded to the superstructure sides, glacis, gun mantlet and barrel to hold foliage camouflage. This modification was apparently common within the battalion and can also be seen in the photographs of the Jagdpanther on the following page.

Photographed on 15 March 1945, after the fighting in the Reichswald, this Jagdpanther also has the metal loops welded to the mantlet, barrel and hull side that can be seen on the vehicle of 2.Kompanie, schwere Panzerjäger-Abteilung 655 depicted in the photograph on the previous page. A company number, which may be 212, is just discernable below the Balkenkreuz on the superstructure side in the photograph above.

116.PANZER-DIVISION

The first battalion of the division's Panzer-Regiment 16 had formed part of Panzer-Brigade 111 until late September 1944 when it returned to its parent formation. Badly depleted, Panzer-Regiment 16 was rebuilt in November and was made up of I.Abteilung with four companies of Panthers and II.Abteilung with two companies of Pzkw IV tanks and two companies of Sturmgeschütz III assault guns.

The division took part in the Ardennes Offensive in late 1944 and by January 1945 had been withdrawn to Kleve on the Waal River, east of Nijmegen. From mid-February, Panzer-Regiment 16 was involved in the defence of the Roer dams until 5 March 1945, when the last Wehrmacht units in the area retreated across the Rhine into Germany. A total of fifteen Jagdpanthers that had originally

been allocated to Nachschub West (1) on 27 March 1945 were later redirected to I.Abteilung, Panzer-Regiment 16 which was at that time near Marl, about 20 kilometres north-west of Dortmund. It is not certain when these vehicles were actually delivered and almost nothing is known about their deployment. In early April 1945 the division was holding the defensive line along the Rhine-Hern canal on the northern edge of the Ruhr valley. Trapped in the pocket created here by the advance of the US 9th Army, the division surrendered on 18 April 1945.

Interestingly, the first battalion was also issued with four Sturmtigers which were first used in combat after the evacuation of Kirchhellen in late March 1945 where one devastating salvo was enough to hold up an American armoured column for several hours.

Notes

1. Nachschub West was the army's supply directorate for the Western Front.

PANZER-LEHR-DIVISION

The division was formed in late 1943 in large part from the staff of various training establishments and famously fought in the battles for Normandy where it was almost annihilated. Although severely depleted, the division was reinforced in August 1944 and fought in the retreat to the Westwall and the Siegfried Line battles in Luxembourg. Partially rebuilt in November, the division returned to the front where it took part in the attempts to halt the advance of the US 3rd Army in the Saar region. The struggle in Normandy had, however, taken its toll and Panzer-Lehr-Division was no longer the superb fighting formation that had arrived in France in early 1944. Indeed, the commander of Heeresgruppe G, General Hermann Balck, had so little faith in the division that he reinforced it with elements of 25.Panzergrenadier-Division which, in fact, saved the Panzer-Lehr division from encirclement. In December 1944, the division was involved in the Ardennes Offensive where, as part of XXXXVII.Panzerkorps, it failed to take the town of Bastogne, a key road junction which was vital to the American defence.

On 10 February 1945, ten Jagdpanthers were allocated to the second company of I.Abteilung, Panzer-Lehr-Regiment. Almost nothing is known of the fate of these vehicles and it is assumed that they were lost in the battles for the Remagen bridgehead or in the Ruhr Pocket. In late March 1945 the surviving tanks were concentrated in I.Abteilung while the Panzer crews without vehicles and the men of the maintenance company were formed into a new II.Abteilung and sent to the Panzertruppen-Schule at Bergen under the command of Hauptmann Freiherr von Schlippenbach (1).

Despite the efforts of the commandant at Bergen to incorporate Schlippenbach's men into his command, an order from

Berlin directed the Panzer-Lehr tankers to the MIAG factory in Braunschweig, where they were to pick up thirty-five new Jagdpanthers, and from there to report to the commanding officer of Werhkreis XI in Hannover (2).

On 7 April 1945 the crews familiarised themselves with their new vehicles and calibrated the guns. The companies, numbered from 5 to 8, received eight Jagdpanthers each while the Stabskompanie was allocated three vehicles. All were the G2 version produced from December 1944.

During the day Schlippenbach conferred with the local commander and although he later claimed to have serious misgivings about any attempt to halt the Allied units advancing towards Braunschweig, he led his men towards the area between Edemissen and Burgdorf, about 35 kilometres west of the city, where a defensive line had been established. The Jagdpanthers were in position that night with the fifth company on the right and the eighth company on the left. Here they remained until 11 April when forward elements of the US 11th Cavalry Regiment ran into the Jagdpanthers of 8.Kompanie and in the ensuing battle Hauptmann von Schlippenbach was incapacitated and Oberleutnant von Falkenhayn assumed command.

Although the forces involved in this battle were relatively small, the fighting was no less ferocious. By the afternoon, two Jagdpanthers had secured the bridge over the Oker at Meinwesen as another was destroyed by a US fighter-bomber. On the fifth company's flank at Edemissen two Jagdpanthers were able to hold up the US 5th Armored Division for two hours until they were forced to retire.

Notes

1. Some accounts record Schlippenbach as the leader of the regiment's second battalion but Helmut Ritgen, who served with the division, lists the Hauptmann as the commander of the Versorgungskompanie from December 1944 until the end of the war.

2. These vehicles had been originally been allocated to 2.Panzer-Division but a total lack of rail transport made their delivery impossible. Germany was divided into several Werhkreis, or military districts, and each was responsible for recruiting, administration and supply. By this stage of the war they were conducting their own defence.

Notes

1. An extra dramatic touch was added by the Feldwebel's name which can be literally translated as fire arrow.

At about noon, elements of SS-Kampfgruppe Wiking passed through the Panzer-Lehr position and made contact with a platoon under the command of Feldwebel Feuerpfeil near the village of Abbensen. After refusing an order to accompany the Wiking Jagdpanthers towards Uetze, a few kilometres to the north, the platoon commander returned his men to the fight.

That night Oberleutnant von Falkenhayn conferred with his company commanders and almost all felt that a continuation of the struggle was senseless. Falkenhayn gave his men permission to make their way home after first destroying their vehicles and any equipment which might benefit the enemy.

However, at least nine crews under the command of a young Leutnant were determined to fight on and on 12 April 1945 made their way into Wendesberg, about 7 kilometres to the north-west of Braunschweig. Here they found that any escape to the north was blocked by large concentrations of enemy troops while to the south the bridges over the Weser-Elbe canal had all been destroyed. Only a small bridge over the Oker remained and it was not strong enough to hold the weight of a Jagdpanther.

After destroying their vehicles, the men split up to make their way to safety as best they could. Another two Jagdpanthers under the command of the redoubtable Feldwebel Feuerpfeil almost managed to reach the Elbe, destroying a number of US Sherman tanks on the way, before they too abandoned their vehicles (1).

A single Jagdpanther, commanded by Feldwebel Stock, was able to reach Rogätz, some 20 kilometres north-east of Magdeburg, during the night of 12 April 1945 and took part in the defence of the city on the following day until it was overwhelmed.

II.Abteilung, Panzer-Lehr-Regiment 130. April 1945

The company numbers were applied in a variety of styles, some quite roughly as can be seen in our illustration on page 24. Photograph evidence is sparse but it is known that the markings of 7.Kompanie consisted of small white numbers painted towards the rear of the superstructure side.

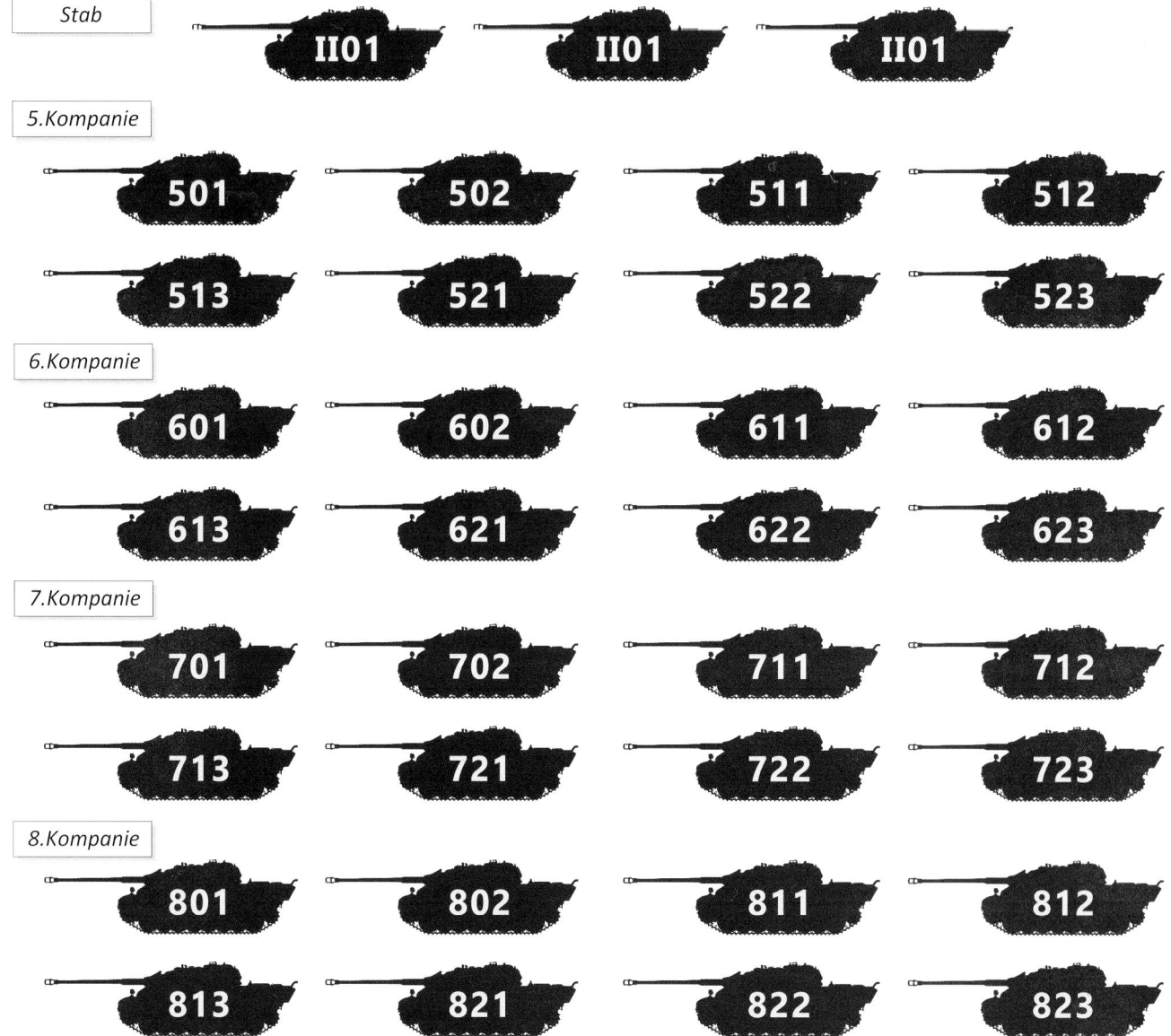

Stab	II01	II01	II01
5.Kompanie	501	502	511	512
	513	521	522	523
6.Kompanie	601	602	611	612
	613	621	622	623
7.Kompanie	701	702	711	712
	713	721	722	723
8.Kompanie	801	802	811	812
	813	821	822	823

Both images here depict the same Jagdpanther of 8.Kompanie, II.Abteilung, Panzer-Lehr-Regiment photographed in late April 1945 after the battalion had surrendered. This vehicle is also discussed on page 24. The company number of 823 is clearly visible in the photograph at left.

PANZER-DIVISION CLAUSEWITZ

This formation was the last armoured division raised by Germany during the war, although it never exceeded the strength of a strong brigade. Formed from parts of badly-depleted units and various training establishments, the division was issued five Jagdpanthers on 14 April 1945 by the Heereszeugamt and these were allocated to the division's Panzer-Abteilung 2106, which had been part of Panzer-Brigade 106 Feldherrnhalle.

By 16 April 1945, just two of the Jagdpanthers were considered operational and these were sent into action in the area east of Lüneburg with ten Panthers against units of the US 5th Armored Division. In the ensuing battle the Americans claimed that they were able to destroy one of the Jagdpanthers, an armoured halftrack and two trucks. It is quite possible that the Jagdpanthers had only arrived on the day before this action took place. A report compiled by the division's headquarters for the following day, 17 April 1945, mentions that Panzer-Abteilung 2106 was composed of one Panzer-Kompanie equipped with Sturmgeschütz IV assault guns and a Gemischtes-Kompanie made up of Panther tanks and Jagdpanthers. Although no numbers are given we can safely assume that some vehicles had survived to this date at least. However, I have been unable to find an account of the action at Fallersleben, where most of the battalion's armoured vehicles were lost on 21 April, that mentions Jagdpanthers. A report written in February 1946 by the division's former commander, Generalmajor Martin Unrein, describes the formation's armoured assets in general terms only as either tanks or assault guns.

The suggestion in some accounts that a number of the division's armoured vehicles were equipped with infra-red sighting equipment is almost certainly incorrect. Although a number of Panthers were fitted with the devices, and the necessary brackets and stowage boxes are clearly visible in surviving photographs, there is no record that any were used in combat in the west. Indeed, the Germans believed that British and American tanks were fitted with sights that could, in complete darkness, detect the infra-red signal.

3.PANZERGRENADIER-DIVISION

The last Kriegsgliederung, or order of battle chart, known to have been made for 3.Panzergrenadier-Division, dated 1 March 1945, contains the notation '1 Jagdpanther 8.8cm' inscribed next to the headquarters of the division's Panzerjäger-Abteilung 3. However, no further mention is made of this vehicle in any other surviving documentation and its origin, and ultimate fate, remain a mystery. On 15 March 1945 the division reported that twenty Pz IV/70 tank destroyers were on hand with the Panzerjäger battalion with nine Sturmgeschütz assault guns and a single Pzkw IV tank with Panzer-Abteilung 103.

SCHWERE PANZER-ABTEILUNG 507

Notes

1. It is not clear who led the company at this time as Oberleutnant Wirsching left the battalion to take command of 1.Kompanie, schwere Panzerjäger-Abteilung 653 in late March 1945. He may have been replaced by Leutnant Bernhard Pfeuffer, one of his platoon commanders.

In early 1945, the battalion was attached to 2.Armee near Zichenau, modern day Ciechanów in Poland, and by the end of January had retreated to the Vistula estuary, losing nineteen tanks in the process although most were destroyed by their own crews. During the second week of February 1945 the battalion's second and third companies were withdrawn to Truppenübungsplatz Sennelager in Germany to be re-equipped with the Tiger II, while 1.Kompanie remained at the front with just two operational tanks. By this time the situation had become so desperate that the companies in training were thrown into the fighting against the US Army which was advancing into central Germany. In early March 1945, three Jagdpanthers were received and these were handed over to 2.Kompanie, commanded by Oberleutnant Dr. Maximilian Wirsching. The exact date the Jagdpanthers were received is, however, uncertain and their origin is also obscure. A total of sixty-eight vehicles were allocated by the Heereszeugamt in February 1945 and a further twenty-four in the following March and all of these seem to be accounted for. Wolfgang Schneider, in his comprehensive histories of the Tiger battalions, states that the Jagdpanthers were received on 9 March 1945 and mentions the second company Jagdpanthers as being in action on the last day of the month. It is entirely possible, although far from certain, that these Jagdpanthers were appropriated from the Sennelager training facility. On 30 March 1945 parts of 2.Kompanie supported SS-Regiment Holzer, part of SS-Brigade Westfalen, in an attack west of Dörenhagen and late in the day took up defensive positions in a wooded area near Dahl and after refuelling moved on to Bad Driburg, about 10 kilometres east of Paderborn. Early on the following day 2.Kompanie, with four Tigers and three Jagdpanthers, attacked enemy positions between Altenbeken and Hamborn, losing three of the Tigers in an ambush (1). In the following days the battalion attempted to halt the advance of the US 3rd Armored Division and by 2 April 1945, most of the battalion's tanks had been dispersed and attached to several Kampfgruppen. On 7 April one of the second company's Jagdpanthers and a single Tiger engaged a US armoured unit near Polle and, firing across the Weser River, managed to destroy seventeen American tanks. Later that day a Jagdpanther was lost and this may have been the last of the original three as no further mention is made of these vehicles in any account I have been able to examine. Indeed, the two Tigers which took part in the defence of the Leine bridge near Göttingen on 9 April are recorded as the battalion's last surviving armoured vehicles. By 17 April 1945 what remained of the battalion had been moved to Prague to be rebuilt and rearmed with Jagdpanzer 38 Hetzer tank destroyers, although it seems that only 3.Kompanie received their allocation. Fighting their way towards the west the survivors of schwere Panzer-Abteilung 507 surrendered to US Army units at Rosenthal, today Rozmitál in the Czech Republic, on 12 May 1945 but were all handed back to the Soviets.

Photographed at Altenkirchen, 35 kilometres north-east of Remagen, in late March 1945 this vehicle was probably from Schwere Panzerjäger-Abteilung 654 or II.Abteilung, Panzer-Lehr-Regiment.

Said to have been photographed in Hannover in 1945 after the city was surrendered to the US 84th Infantry Division, this Jagdpanther is typical of late-production MNH vehicles. It would be tempting to speculate that this is one of the Jagdpanthers of SS-Kampfgruppe Wiking but none were lost within the city.

SS-KAMPFGRUPPE WIKING

This company-sized battle group was the only formation of the SS-Wiking division to serve in the west during the course of the war and the only unit of the Waffen-SS to operate Jagdpanthers on the Western Front and as such it deserves to be examined in some detail. On 2 April 1945, about 150 Panzer crewmen of SS-Panzer-Regiment 5 under the commander of Hauptsturmführer Karl Nicolussi-Leck were ordered to Paderborn in Germany to pick up a number of new tanks.

An advance party led by Obersturmführer Ulf-Ola Olin ran into the lead elements of the US 5th Armored Division near in Harsewinkel, a small town between Münster and Bielefeld, and were forced to retreat to Lübbecke and then to Minden, which they found to be under attack by the British.

Finding a number of vehicles along the way, including two SdKfz 250/9 halftracks armed with 2cm guns, they were finally joined by Nicolussi-Leck and the remainder of the company on 7 April 1945, in Hannover. Here the garrison commander, Generalmajor Paul Löhning, ordered them to take up defensive positions along Reichsstrasse 6, which runs north towards Bremen, in anticipation of an American attack. On the following morning Nicolussi-Leck learnt from a local civilian that a number of armoured vehicles were sitting in the nearby MNH assembly plant at Hannover-Laatzen and rushing to the factory he found seven Jagdpanthers (1).

He immediately set about organising crews for each vehicle and sent out search parties to acquire fuel, spare parts and ammunition while the Jagdpanther crews used the time to calibrate and test-fire their guns. Using his own initiative, a trait for which he was justly famous,

Hauptsturmführer Nicolussi-Leck ordered his men to move forward from their assigned positions to Frielingen and Ricklingen where they were able to cover the approaches to the Leine bridge and Bordenau. The first American attacks were directed at Ricklingen where they were met by three Jagdpanthers which were only dislodged, without loss, after an intense artillery bombardment. In an attempt to outflank the German defenders the American commander sent a force to Bordenau, where the British already held the bridge, but this was met by another four Jagdpanthers. As night fell the Americans had made little headway for the loss of over twenty armoured vehicles while Nicolussi-Leck had lost a single Jagdpanther and one of the halftracks. The fighting continued on the next day with the Jagdpanthers destroying three Sherman tanks. However, the forces available for the defence of Hannover could not hope to hold out indefinitely and on the same day Generalmajor Löhning asked for permission to abandon the city.

On 10 April, after a prolonged artillery barrage, the American units resumed their assault and aided by the thick fog which enveloped the battlefield, the attackers managed to infiltrate the German lines and bypass the vehicles of Kampfgruppe Wiking. A single Jagdpanther, which had been parked in the autobahn underpass on Reichsstrasse 6, was surrounded and captured without a fight, its crew apparently asleep. Two US Army regiments continued into Hannover and took the city almost unopposed. Unaware that the garrison had surrendered and unable to make contact with any German units, Nicolussi-Leck ordered his men to withdraw into Hannover. Although the Americans had by this time had been able to occupy

Notes

1. Some sources give a figure of eight, however, I am convinced that the number mentioned here is correct.

Notes

1. Although Wittenberge, the location given in most German accounts, was a major transport hub and strongly defended, it is over 100 kilometres from Hannover and so far east that it was by this time being overflown by Russian reconnaissance aircraft. It is possible that Nicolussi-Leck meant Wittingen which was on the same route, much closer and still in German hands.

2. Ulf-Ola Olin was a Finnish volunteer and one of the few Finns who remained with the Waffen-SS when his country negotiated a separate peace with the Soviet Union.

large parts of the city, the Jagdpanthers and other vehicles of Kampfgruppe Wiking managed to pass through Hannover and after a number of close scrapes, headed towards the east in the hope of finding the German lines. On the next day Nicolussi-Leck turned his Kampfgruppe north and then north-east towards Wittenberge on the Elbe River (1).

Unknown to the Germans they were moving almost parallel to elements of the US 84th Infantry Division on converging routes which met at Langlingen, 5 kilometres south-east of Celle. Along the way the Jagdpanthers were involved in a brief firefight with four Sherman tanks, destroying two of them, and near Uetze, captured two US Army fuel trucks and fifty men. Having no facilities to deal with prisoners Nicolussi-Leck freed them during the hours of darkness.

On 12 April 1945, Kampfgruppe Wiking with six Jagdpanthers was sheltered in the forest east of Sandlingen, just to the east of the Celle to Braunschweig road. Finding that the bridges near Langlingen had been destroyed, Nicolussi-Leck sent a halftrack towards Wienhausen in an attempt to find an intact bridge across the Aller River, which they did at about 2.00pm at Oppershausen. At almost the same time infantrymen of the US 333rd Regiment entered Wienhausen, less than a kilometre to the north-east, and turning towards Oppershausen noticed the German halftrack which they immediately brought under fire. At first the Germans assumed they were being attacked by their own men and an army Feldwebel was killed as he attempted to approach the Americans. Realising their mistake the remaining Germans set off the demolition charges that had been left at the bridge and managed to hold off the Americans for nine hours while the village of Oppershausen was destroyed around them. Although the halftrack crew displayed exemplary courage in hanging on to their position, Kampfgruppe Wiking's last escape route had been closed with the destruction of the bridge.

On Friday, 13 April Nicolussi-Leck told Obersturmführer Olin that he intended to remain in hiding until the advance American units had moved out of the area and then search for a crossing of the Aller, avoiding a fight wherever possible. However, US Army engineers had discovered a repairable bridge and patrols sent out from their defensive perimeter came into contact with parts of Kampfgruppe Wiking. In the course of a short exchange of fire American reinforcements arrived and before long the Germans were massively outnumbered. Nicolussi-Leck ordered his men to withdraw towards the north-west and the town of Wienhausen where they ran head-on into an enemy artillery battalion that was hurrying to a position from which they hoped to fire on the retreating Germans. The Jagdpanthers opened fire at a range of 1,000 metres destroying five trucks in the first salvo and forcing the Americans to retire. Reaching Wienhausen the Germans were advised of a ford just outside the town and the Jagdpanthers were able to cross the river, reaching the area east of Ostersloh that night, towing two of the halftracks which had broken down.

On the following day the Kampfgruppe continued on towards the east cautiously moving from the shelter of one wooded area to the next. Near Hohne, almost 10 kilometres to the east of Wienhausen, the unmistakeable sounds of a large armoured force on the move could be heard coming from the south. Faced with the prospect of a fight against overwhelming forces and considering the impassable Hahnenmoor bog ahead of him, Nicolussi-Leck decided that his only option was to head north and steal past the Americans between Hohne and Ummern. With three Jagdpanthers in the lead, and three more covering the advance, the Germans suddenly came under fire from twenty US Army Shermans which destroyed two halftracks and a Jagdpanther. One of the forward Jagdpanthers broke through and continued onwards but was not seen again. Untersturmführer Karl Jauss, who had been with the regiment since its formation in late 1943, attempted to recover one of the burning Jagpanthers but this only resulted in the loss of the battle group's only Bergepanzer. However, the 8.8cm guns of the remaining Jagdpanthers were by now pouring a murderous fire into the Shermans and when Nicolussi-Leck withdrew his men into the relative safety of the Hahnenmoor bog it must have been to the great relief of the American tankers. That night the Germans managed to captured two US Army trucks, thinking they were transporting fuel, only to find that they contained flour and sugar. With almost no ammunition, little fuel and down to thirty men the Germans realised that they had no hope of regaining their own lines.

On the morning of 16 April 1945, Nicolussi-Leck, leaving Obersturmführer Olin in command, made his way to the American lines to surrender (2). In his absence the two captured trucks were burned while the last two Jagdpanthers were driven into a bog where they sank under their own weight. Despite a search, no trace has ever been found of either. The remaining ammunition, just ten rounds, was buried nearby.

The Jagdpanther that had broken through at Hohne two days previously was isolated and knocked out in the area between Süderwittingen and Ohrdorf, five kilometres South of Wittingen, on the same day the Kampfgruppe surrendered.

PANZER-STÜTZPUNKT MAYEN

The German Army established a number of support bases, or Stützpunkte, whose function was to administer the supply of vehicles, spare parts and other necessary materials. These bases were normally set up at rail or road junctions behind the front and were often of a temporary nature, particularly late in the war. On 29 January 1945, ten Jagdpanthers were allocated to the Panzer-Stützpunkt located at Mayen, approximately 20 kilometres west of Koblenz in western Germany. These vehicles quite probably came from schwere Panzerjäger-Abteilung 654 and may have been the Jagdpanthers dispatched by the Heereszeugamt to the battalion on 25 January. What became of these vehicles is not known although they certainly did not take part in the defence of the town. On 8 March 1945 a task force from the US 11th Armored Division captured Mayen with little difficulty, the division's official history stating that the German defences were overcome by dismounted infantry who faced only small arms fire and the occasional Panzerfaust. Indeed, there is no mention of the division encountering any German armoured vehicles either at Mayen or in the subsequent fighting for Andernach, some 15 kilometres further to the east.

PANZER-EINSATZ-ABTEILUNG 20

Formed from elements of Panzer-Ausbildungs und Ersatz-Abteilung 20, a training and replacement unit based in the Hamburg area, the battalion was made up of a staff and four companies numbered 1, 5, 6 and 9 and a maintenance platoon. The first company, in some documentation referred to as 1.(Sturmgeschütz) Kompanie and also Sturmgeschütz-Kompanie 20, was equipped with a mixture of tanks, tank destroyers and assault guns including two Jagdpanthers which were probably the vehicles allocated to the Ersatzheer by the Heereszeugamt on 15 January 1945. At least one of these Jagdpanthers survived the fighting and was photographed at an Allied vehicle dump at Oldenburg in May 1945. Together with Panzer-Ausbildungs-Abteilung Grossdeutschland, the battalion took part in the fighting along the Weser River and north-western Germany in April 1945 (1).

Notes

1. This unit is referred to in some accounts as Panzer-Einsatz-Abteilung Bauer, after its commanding officer, Hauptmann Bauer.

Photographed at Oldenburg, north-west of Bremen, in May 1945 this may be the only surviving Jagdpanther of Panzer-Einsatz-Abteilung 20. Reporting that two vehicles were on hand with 1.Kompanie on 4 April 1945, the battalion certainly saw combat as the company commander, Oberleutnant Peiper, was killed on the following day. The camouflage is typical of MNH Jagdpanthers assembled from November 1944, although this vehicle appears to have the earlier engine deck suggesting it was manufactured at some time prior to December. It is not certain that the number 59 was applied by the Germans and it would seem to have no connection to the first company.

JAGDPANTHER AUSF G1

At right: A January 1944 production vehicle featuring the single-piece gun barrel with early muzzle brake (1), cylindrical container for the gun cleaning rods (2), early exhausts (3), Panther ausf A rear deck (4) and Scheinwerfer (5). Note that the tool rack is set at an angle, a common feature of vehicles assembled by MIAG.

Notes

1) The expression Fahrgestell, or Fgst, refers to the chassis and each vehicle was identified by a Fahrgestellnummer, or chassis number. The first Jagdpanther was numbered 300001.

2. The air-intake louvres behind the superstructure were also slightly narrower.

In January 1944, just two months behind schedule, the first of the production Jagdpanthers left the assembly lines at the Mühlenbau und Industrie AG (MIAG) plant in Braunschweig. It is unlikely that the name Jagdpanther was in use at the time and, to the best of our knowledge, the vehicles were referred to as schwere Panzerjäger (Fahrgestell Panther mit 8.8cm) (1). These early vehicles had two driver's periscopes in the glacis covered by a rain guard in the shape of an inverted V and the smaller, internally-bolted Geschütznische or gun recess (A).

On the superstructure roof, the periscope guards were the 110mm tall version (B), while the loader's rotatable periscope had a 20mm thick base and the rotating plate for the commander's periscope was mounted higher than the cast armour base (C).

As the rear deck was based on the Panther ausf A it retained the antenna base, although it was relocated to the right hand side, and also a metal cap over the air intake aperture (2).

The rear stowage bins were also the same as those used on the Panther ausf A and were mounted on a curved base plate and hung from leather straps over the hull rear plate. Many other features were lifted straight for the Panther programme including the road wheels with twenty-four reinforcing bolts, the drive sprocket and strengthened rear idler and the Scheinwerfer, or headlight. The 15-ton jack was stored horizontally and held by hangers bolted to the exhaust guards. In addition, the first fifty production vehicles to leave the assembly lines were built with a 16mm thick roof plate which was later

replaced by a plate of 25mm thickness. The tool rack on the left side of the hull was fitted with a tube to hold the towing cable and held a towing clevis, wire cutters and a shovel. The right side rack was similarly constructed and held a clevis, a fire extinguisher, an axe and a starter crank. Behind the rack, a bracket was welded to the hull for the wooden jack block and next to that was a holder for the track replacement cable. On the same side, towards the rear another rack held the track tensioning tool, a hammer and a wrecking bar.

Racks to carry spare track links were welded to both sides at the rear. The first vehicles issued to units in the field were all fitted with hull Schürzen.

From the commencement of production until the end of the war all the armoured hulls, or Panzer wanne, were constructed by Brandenburger Eisenwerke while the final assembly was undertaken by MIAG. From November 1944, as a temporary expedient, the firms of Maschinenfabrik Niedersachsen Hannover (MNH) and Maschinenfabrik Bahn Bedarf (MBA) were both contracted to assemble the Jagdpanther.

A number of modifications were incorporated into the manufacturing process until production ceased in April 1945 and most of these are listed below.

Note that I have not included some internal and mechanical changes nor unofficial modifications made by units in the field. A number of the latter were identifying features of certain formations and are discussed with the colour illustrations of the Camouflage and Markings section.

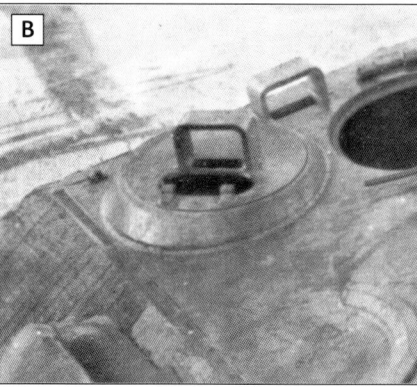

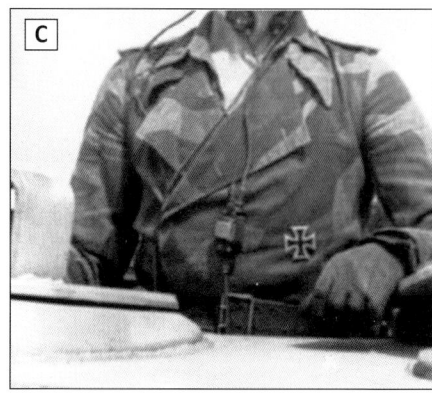

January 1944. The five pistol ports fitted to the prototypes were not included on production vehicles but were replaced by the Nahverteidigungswaffe close-defence weapon which was mounted in the roof (A). As with the Panther, production delays meant that it was not fitted until June 1944 and vehicles assembled before that time had a circular plate with four bolts covering the aperture for the Nahverteidigungswaffe. From the first production vehicle, Jagdpanthers were equipped with Kgs 64/660/150 track links with six chevrons cast into the track face, which improved traction (B). All vehicles are coated with Zimmerit anti-magnetic mine paste before leaving the factory (C).

February 1944. It is likely that the first Befehls-Jagdpanthers were built during this month.

March 1944. The vehicle is referred to in official documentation as Jagdpanther (8,8cm Pak43/3 L/71 auf Fgst. Panther I). Three metal rods or spikes were welded to the roof in front of the loader's position to hold the tripod mount of the EM 0.9 R rangefinder with which each vehicle was equipped.

April 1944. The sectional barrel began to replace the single-piece version (D). Both were referred to as 8.8cm Pak 43/3. The holes for the antenna base and air intake were no longer cut into the rear deck.

May 1944. A towing coupling was welded to the inspection port on the hull rear plate below the exhaust covers (E). Consequently the jack was now mounted vertically between the exhaust mufflers (F). Welded, rectangular armoured guards for the exhausts began to replace the cast models. Near the end of the Jagdpanther production run a simpler square version was introduced.

June 1944. The second driver's periscope on the glacis was dropped from production. Many hulls had been built with the necessary hole and these were covered with a metal plate and welded shut (G). These plates are difficult, if not impossible, to detect on vehicles coated with Zimmerit. Self cleaning idler wheels are introduced although the older models were still being fitted in February 1945 when stocks were exhausted (H). A lighter muzzle brake, originally designed for the Pak 43/41, was introduced for the 8.8cm gun, however, the older version was still being fitted as late as October (I). Three sockets, or Pilze, were welded to the roof to accommodate the 2-ton Behelfkran jib boom. The sockets were mounted at the centre of the roof at the front with one in each corner at the rear. Interestingly, MIAG used Pilze of their own design, which were noticeably shorter, and MNH did not fit any. The installation of the Nahverteidigungswaffe began.

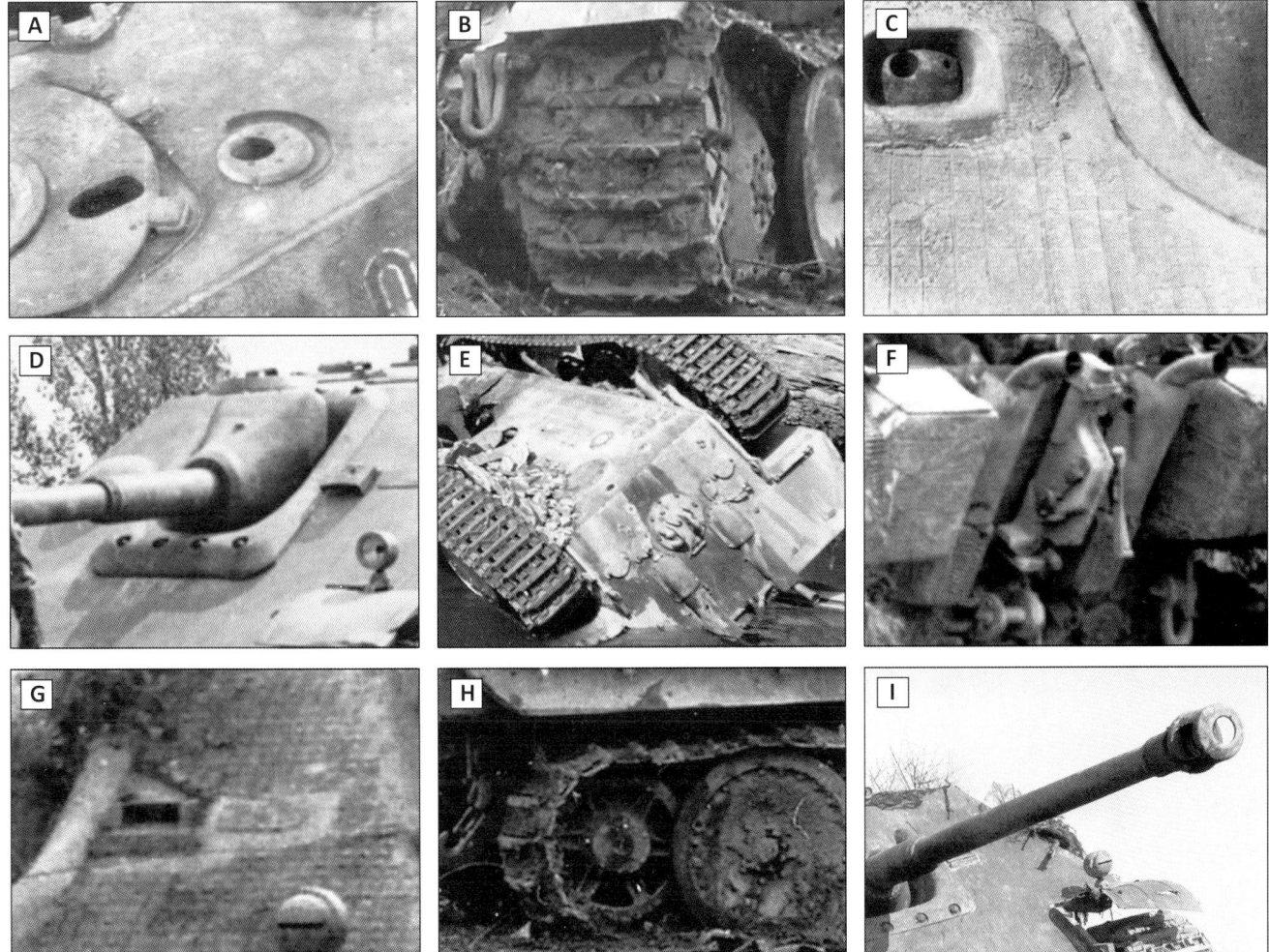

July 1944. Two additional cooling pipes were added to the left-hand side exhaust in an effort to stop the left cylinder bank overheating (A). By this time, track links manufactured by August Engels Eissengiesseherei, with which most Jagdpanthers were fitted, were cast with a spike on the left end of each link. The Panther ausf G rear stowage bins replaced the Panther ausf A versions. Two U-shaped brackets were welded to the hull rear to hold the towing cables.

August 1944. The Topfblende gun mantlet was cast with a boss which was drilled to create a lifting eye.

September 1944. The application of Zimmerit was discontinued early in the month.

October 1944. A completely re-designed, thicker Geschütznische was introduced into production. The Panther ausf A Kugelblende machine-gun mount was replaced by a version with a stepped aperture. By the end of the Jagdpanther's production run a model with a flatter profile was being fitted. A new pattern rear stowage bin with five raised ribs on its outer face was introduced into production. Photographic evidence would suggest that very few of these were fitted to Jagdpanthers (B). Sheet metal guards were mounted around the exhaust pipes in an effort to conceal the very obvious glow at night (C). These should not be confused with the Flammvernichter mufflers mentioned below. The last of the single-piece barrels were probably fitted at this time.

November 1944. The width of the metal rain guard was increased from 206mm to 226mm. A new type of towing shackle was issued.

December 1944. Over the previous two months a total of ten Jagdpanthers built at MNH had the air intake vent located at the front of the roof, directly over the main gun. On all other production vehicles this intake vent, and its armoured cover, was situated behind the driver's hatch. Troops in the field were ordered to construct protective covers for the louvres and air intakes of the rear deck from pieces of Schürzen. Production of a new hull with the Panther ausf G engine deck probably began at this time.

January 1945. The first Jagdpanthers with the new hull are probably assembled at this time.

The Jagdpanther of Major Erich Sattler, disabled at Hectrel in Belgium on 8 September 1944. Built by MIAG in July 1944 this vehicle has the later 25mm thick roof, and interestingly, a mixture of the 110mm and 100mm tall periscope guards. The porcelain insulator for the Sternantenna is visible here in its armoured cover.

February 1945. A third stowage box, mounted at the rear of the fighting compartment, was deleted from production, probably due to a lack of components. These boxes were almost identical to the field-modified examples used by schwere Panzerjäger-Abteilung 654 from April 1944 (A). It is not certain when they were first incorporated in general production and may only have been fitted to MNH-built Jagdpanthers which would mean that fewer than eighty vehicles could have had the extra boxes.

March/April 1945. On MNH-assembled Jagdpanthers the return roller was replaced by a skid shoe (B). Almost at the end of production, the machined cap of the drive sprocket was replaced by a cast, armoured version (C).

JAGDPANTHER AUSF G2

At right: A March/April 1945 production vehicle featuring the raised tower for the crew compartment heater (1) and Flammvernichter mufflers (2). Note the large pin welded to the hull front (3), the self-cleaning rear idler (4) and scoop behind the Kampfraumheizung (5).

In late 1944, probably in December, the Brandenburger Eisenwerke began to construct the Panzerwanne with an engine compartment layout almost identical to that of the Panther ausf G in order to accommodate an internal change to the engine cooling system (1).

The rear deck was now about 20mm longer and this necessitated a change to the shape of the superstructure which was in fact so slight that it is difficult to identify in contemporary photographs. The most obvious difference was the addition of the raised tower for the crew compartment heater (2) and also the elimination of the two louvres at each side of the engine deck at the rear. The latter were replaced by smaller air intakes and their function of regulating the radiator water temperature was achieved by adjusting the sliding sheet metal covers which were now fitted over both right-hand side intakes.

These changes to the engine cooling system meant that the twin pipes on the left-hand exhaust were no longer needed and new mufflers referred to as Flammvernichter were introduced which solved the problem of the glowing exhausts and also prevented backfires (3). Curiously some vehicles were fitted with both the cooling pipes and the later Flammvernichter mufflers. Most of the tool racks and tools were moved from the sides to the rear although the jack block and its bracket were still fitted to the right side and the container for the gun cleaning rods was also retained. In place of the tool racks, a large metal pin was welded to the hull front to hold the towing cable which was fastened at the rear by a metal pipe fixed to the rack for the spare tracks. On the superstructure roof a pivoting driver's periscope replaced the cast armour guard behind the curved armoured cover for the sight hole. It is likely that the first 300 production Jagdpanthers were completed with the initial Panther ausf A rear deck before the changes to the Panzerwanne took place and as a considerable number of hulls had already been delivered, and three firms were by this time involved in the manufacture of the Jagdpanther, it is almost certain that assembly of both types continued, perhaps side by side, until the end of the war (4). The changes affecting internal painting and also camouflage colours applied to all Panzers.

It should be mentioned that the very existence of the Jagdpanther G2, or at least the designation, rests on the evidence of a letter of 27 February 1945 from MNH to the army's acceptance inspector which mentions the Jagdpanther G1, which is taken to mean the vehicle with the Panther ausf A rear engine deck.

Notes

1) The first hull may have been completed in December but is unlikely that any complete vehicles were assembled before January 1945.

2. The internal heater or Kampfraumheizung had been fitted to the Panther since October 1944.

2. The new exhaust mufflers were incorporated into the production of the Panther ausf G from October 1944.

3. Brandenburger Eisenwerke is known to have completed at least 795 Panzerwanne before the end of the war. This means that perhaps slightly more than half the total number were assembled into complete vehicles.

Dragon Models Ltd
B1-10/F., 603-609 Castle Peak Rd.
Kong Nam Industrial Building
Tsuen Wan, N. T., Hong Kong (of China).
www.dragon-models.com

Dragon USA
1315 John Reed Ct, City of Industry,
CA 91745, USA
www.dragonmodelsusa.com

Tamiya Inc
Shizuoka City, Japan
www.tamiya.com

Airfix
www.airfix.com/uk-en/

Revell
www.revell.com/

Royal Model
Via E. Montale, 19-95030 Pedara, Italy
www.royalmodel.com

Italeri S.p.A.
Via Pradazzo 6/b
40012 Calderara di Reno, Bologna, Italy
www.italeri.com

Jordi Rubio
Carrer de Còrsega, 625, 08025 Barcelona,
Spain
www. Jordirubio.com/en

Archer Fine Transfers
PO Box 1277, Youngsville, NC 27596
USA
www.archertransfers.com

Star Decals
www.star-decals.net
Formerly Bison Decals

Hauler
Jan Sobotka
Moravská 38
620 00 Brno
Czech Republic
www.hauler.cz

Voyager Model
Room 501, No.411 4th Village
SPC Jinshan District
Shanghai 200540
P.R.China
www.voyagermodel.com

Griffon Model
Suite 501, Bldg 01, 418 Middle Longpan
Road, Nanjing, China
www.griffonmodel.com

Aber
ul. Jalowcowa 15, 40-750 Katowice, Poland
www.aber.net.pl

E.T. Models
www.etmodeller.com

Friulmodel
H 8142. Urhida, Nefelejcs u. 2., Hungary
www.friulmodel.hu

Modelkasten
Chiyoda-ku Kanda, Nishiki-Cho 1-7, Tokyo,
Japan
www.modelkasten.com
Very difficult to navigate but worthwhile

Academy Plastic Models
521-1, Yonghyeon-dong, Uijeongbu-si,
Gyeonggi-do, Korea
www.academy.co.kr

ROCHM Model
www.rochmmodel.com
rochmmodel@gmail.com

Eduard Model Accessories
Mirova 170, 435 21 Obrnice
Czech Republic
www.eduard.com

Model Artisan Mori
Yasutsugu Mori
Maison Suiryu 302, Kunoshiro-cho 1-10
Yokkaichi-City, Mie 510-0072, Japan
www.artisanmori.web.fc2.com

RB Model
Powstancow Wlkp.29B
64-360 Zbaszyn
Poland
www.rbmodel.com

Alliance Model Works
No postal addess available at the time of
writing
www.am-works.com

Zvezda (Zvezda-America)
www.zvezda-usa.com

Peddinghaus Decals
www.decals.guenstigergeht.net

Black Dog
Petr Polanka
Letecká 549
Libèice nad Vltavou
252 66, Czech Republic
www.blackdog.cz

GPM Modele Kartonowe
Zacisze 2 95-054 Ksawerow Poland
www.gpm.pl

In compiling this book I have tried to provide the general reader with a guide to understanding what can at times appear a bewildering subject and also to inspire modellers to create a scale representation of what was perhaps the most potent tank destroyer produced by any side during the Second World War. In researching the unit histories and technical information sections I drew heavily on the works of the late Thomas Jentz, including the excellent *Jagdpanther* from the *Panzer Tracts* series and *Panzertruppen Volume 2*, which I would recommend to any reader with an interest in German armour. I would also recommend a number of the books of Karl-Heinz Münch, particularly *The Combat History of the 654th Schwere Panzerjager Abteilung* and *Panzerjager Technical and Operational History* and also *Rüchmarsch! The German Retreat From Normandy* by Jean Paul Pallud, a detailed account of the battles around Falaise and the subsequent withdrawal to the Seine. Worthwhile but difficult to obtain, and available only in German, is *Krieg in der Heimat* by Ulrich Saft. I also drew on my research for *Westwall* and *A Sound Like Thunder* which I wrote in 2011 and 2013 respectively and *Panzers in the Bocage*, written by Karl Berne. I should also acknowledge the contributors to the Axis History and the Feldgrau forums, especially Martin Block and the late Ron Klages whose research on unit histories and vehicle allocations would fill many volumes and also the contributors to Brett Green's Missing Lynx discussion forum. Of the product manufacturers I must make special mention of Roberto Reale of Royal Model, Jan Zdiarsky from Eduard Accessories and Freddie Leung of Dragon Models who all helped enormously. As always, I am indebted to my good friends Karl Berne, Valeri Polokov and J.Howard Parker for their invaluable assistance with the photographs and period insignia. Lastly, I would like to thank the extremely talented modellers who generously allowed me to publish the images of their work, particularly Bernard Cher of MWorkshop, who brought many of them together, and Rupert Harding and Stephen Chumbley at Pen & Sword for their advice, assistance and patience.

ALSO AVAILABLE IN THE TANKCRAFT SERIES